THE MORAL VOYAGES OF STEPHEN KING

MORE WILDSIDE CLASSICS

Dacobra, or The White Priests of Ahriman, by Harris Burland
The Nabob, by Alphonse Daudet
Out of the Wreck, by Captain A. E. Dingle
The Elm-Tree on the Mall, by Anatole France
The Lance of Kanana, by Harry W. French
Amazon Nights, by Arthur O. Friel
Caught in the Net, by Emile Gaboriau
The Gentle Grafter, by O. Henry
Raffles, by E. W. Hornung
Gates of Empire, by Robert E. Howard
Tom Brown's School Days, by Thomas Hughes
The Opium Ship, by H. Bedford Jones
The Miracles of Antichrist, by Selma Lagerlof
Arsène Lupin, by Maurice LeBlanc
A Phantom Lover, by Vernon Lee
The Iron Heel, by Jack London
The Witness for the Defence, by A.E.W. Mason
The Spider Strain and Other Tales, by Johnston McCulley
Tales of Thubway Tham, by Johnston McCulley
The Prince of Graustark, by George McCutcheon
Bull-Dog Drummond, by Cyril McNeile
The Moon Pool, by A. Merritt
The Red House Mystery, by A. A. Milne
Blix, by Frank Norris
Wings over Tomorrow, by Philip Francis Nowlan
The Devil's Paw, by E. Phillips Oppenheim
Satan's Daughter and Other Tales, by E. Hoffmann Price
The Insidious Dr. Fu Manchu, by Sax Rohmer
Mauprat, by George Sand
The Slayer and Other Tales, by H. de Vere Stacpoole
Penrod (Gordon Grant Illustrated Edition), by Booth Tarkington
The Gilded Age, by Mark Twain
The Blockade Runners, by Jules Verne
The Gadfly, by E.L. Voynich

Please see www.wildsidepress.com for a complete list!

THE MORAL VOYAGES OF STEPHEN KING

by

ANTHONY MAGISTRALE

WILDSIDE PRESS

For Jennifer — who enabled me to find the time to write, and inspired me with the will to do so.

Copyright © 1898 by Starmont House, Inc.
All rights reserved. International copyright reserved in all countries. No part of this book may be reproduced in any form, except for brief passages quoted in reviews, with the expressed written permission of the publisher.

THE MORAL VOYAGES OF STEPHEN KING

This edition published in 2006 by Wildside Press, LLC.
www.wildsidepress.com

Table of Contents

Introduction i

Chapter 1
Moral Collapse: Character, Setting,
Free Will and Tragic Designs 1

Part One:
When Good and Evil Collide 25

Chapter 2
The Devil in the Machine:
Technological Boogeymen 27

Chapter 3
The Fall from Grace:
Sexuality and the Corruption of Innocence 42

Chapter 4
The Shape Evil Takes:
Hawthorne's Woods Revisited 57

Chapter 5
The Divine and the Damned:
Tom Cullen and Trashcan Man 68

Part Two:
And Those Who Are Left to Tell the Tale 79

Chapter 6
Speculations from the Locker Room:
Male-Bonding and Non-Traditional Families 81

Chapter 7
Giving Birth to Salvation:
The Mystery of Motherhood 93

Chapter 8
Portraits of the Artist:
The Writer as Survivor 106

Works Cited 121

Selected Bibliography 125

INDEX 154

INTRODUCTION

The novel is quite well. What we should perhaps be moaning over is the death of literary criticism in America, the loss of clear, sane voices in the popular periodicals in our time, the snobbishness of those writers who analyze fiction for the small and oppressive, and the really alarming failure of these would-be critics to distinguish between quality and celebrity. To go even a step further, I would suggest a stranger inability: the inability to see that quality and celebrity need not always be mutually exclusive.
--Stephen King, Elliott lecture, University of Maine, Orono, November 6, 1986

Stephen King has reached the point in his career where the sale of books is no longer his major criterion for the measurement of literary success. Indeed, how can mere numbers of volumes sold be viewed as any kind of challenge to an author whose latest work, regardless of genre or its critical reception, is guaranteed to reach the top of the best seller lists in less than a week after publication release?

Stephen King is now looking beyond immediate book sales and toward the future. In his own early morning moments of self-doubt, sitting in his magnificent Victorian mansion in Bangor, Maine, he must sometimes wonder if his fiction will still be read fifty or a hundred years from now.

Late in his recent novel <u>Misery</u>, King's writer-protagonist Paul Sheldon issues a plea for critical acknowledgement, insisting that his work is more than merely the stuff of commercial potboilers and sentimental romances. The critics, he argues, have failed to see

that they were dealing with a young Mailer or Cheever here--that they were dealing with a <u>heavywweight</u> here. As a result, hadn't his 'serious' fiction become steadily more self-conscious, a sort of scream? <u>Look at me! Look how good this is! Hey, guys! This stuff has got a sliding perspective! This stuff has got</u>

i

> steam-of-consciousness interludes! This is my
> REAL WORK, you assholes! Don't you dare turn
> away from me . . . . (264)

In this instance, as well as others throughout the novel, the reader is sorely tempted to identify the author with his character. As the quotation that begins this chapter exemplifies, King is concerned with--and often disappointed by--his reception at the hands of the literary establishment. If left to "those writers who analyze fiction for the small and oppressive," King would indeed remain relegated to the status of popular phenomenon--a slightly extended illustration of Andy Warhol's definition of a fifteen-minute celebrity.

Tim Underwood has co-edited two highly successful collections of critical essays on King's fiction, and in his own concluding entry in Kingdom of Fear, "The Skull Beneath the Skin," he insists that King's

> work probably won't last . . . . Stories like "The Raft" or The Mist may have the power to disturb, but their effects are ephemeral. Neither story resonates in the mind like W.W. Jacob's "The Monkey's Paw," Edgar Allan Poe's "The Premature Burial," J. Sheridan Le Fanu's "The Green Tea," Algernon Blackwood's "August Heat," Shirley Jackson's "The Lottery," or even Oscar Wilde's The Picture of Dorian Grey. (255-256)

Of all King's detractors, Mr. Underwood ought to be more sympathetic, especially in light of his two, generally positive collections assessing King's merits as a fiction writer. One is forced to wonder how carefully Underwood has read the essays written by his contributors. Moreover, the basis and validity for the judgment rendered above must be questioned. Perhaps The Mist is not the most memorable of King's tales, and ultimately may well be deserted and forgotten by future generations. But in citing some of the best tales written by some of the best practitioners of horror fiction in the last two hundred years, Underwood does King a grave disservice by not extending the comparison to King's best work: The Shining, The

Stand, Pet Sematary, The Body. Perhaps Mr. Underwood senses the true strength of these texts and is apprehensive that his argument may be mortally weakened by their inclusion; the King novels cited above certainly are in league with, or better than, any of the fiction Underwood ranks as superior to King's. As a further point of disagreement, I would argue that there is nothing "ephemeral" about the anxieties associated with "The Raft." This is a tale about the terrors of adulthood. The four children who swim out to the raft to give summer one last kiss, find themselves confronting the dark realities of adulthood: the loss of innocence, the betrayal of friendships and love, the inescapable destruction of their youth. There is, then, a sub-text to this gruesome story about a circular membrane that floats. As any college student who has read this tale will tell you, this is as disconcerting a piece of fiction as any King has yet to tell, and it certainly belongs with the best work of Poe or Jackson.

Elsewhere in "The Skull Beneath the Skin" Underwood posits that King's literature is "not primarily concerned with the higher centers of the brain; his aim is visceral" (257). Here Underwood subscribes to a critical lament that has always plagued the horror genre: it's fascination with the grotesque and the gruesome. I can offer little by way of qualifying negative responses to the visceral elements inherent in horror fiction, except to remind the reader that he need search no further than Shakespeare to find a similar fascination often at work.

More important, Underwood grossly simplifies King in assuming that his fiction contains neither complexity nor serious intellectual engagement. This thesis ignores not only important aspects in King's canon, but also those which remain the most interesting. The mutli-leveled relationship between society and the self examined in The Stand, the moral implications of the dialectic between free will and determinism in The Shining, the numerous mythological archetypes that are employed in It, and the association with a Puritan conception of the American frontier and forest in Pet Sematary are just a few possibilities that illustrate specifically where Mr. Underwood has underestimated the intellectual content of King's oeuvre. Unfortunately, King's work probably will not endure if readers continue to remain oblivious to the intellectual substance available in his fiction; unless the very critical establishment that King so frequently lambasts helps to establish the writer as the rightful heir to a literary tradition that includes Poe and Hawthorne, Dickens and Stoker, his contribution is likely destined for the obscurity that awaits most popular forms of entertainment in America.

I raise these issues not in an effort to chastise Tim Underwood or others of his persuasion so much as to justify the existence of my own book. There are a growing number of literary scholars writing about Stephen King--Douglas Winter and Michael Collings are perhaps the most recognizable--who have treated his work to the kind of probing analyses that good literature deserves and requires if it is to be appreciated fully. In <u>The Many Facets of Stephen King</u> and <u>The Shorter Works of Stephen King</u>, Collings has supplied the emerging realm of King scholarship with biographical contexts for comprehending the evolution of his prolific canon, while Douglas Winter's <u>The Art of Darkness</u> continues to be the most accessible and global introduction to the writer's enormous body of fiction.

My goal in writing this book was to continue the advance of this emerging corpus of critical labors by presenting a still more focused approach. The reader will be disappointed if she comes to this volume seeking a comprehensive treatment of the many texts contained in King's canon. I have deliberately narrowed my scope to an examination of several of his paramount literary themes and philosophical concerns. I can only trust that this perspective serves to heighten the reader's appreciation for the material analyzed, and that she will come to join me in recognizing with King himself "that quality and celebrity need not always be mutually exclusive."

This book owes its very existence to a variety of sources. First, I wish to express thanks to Virginia Clark, Chair of the English Department at the University of Vermont, for her resolute commitment to this project from its inception, and, for that matter, for her support for nearly everything I have endeavored to accomplish since joining her departmental faculty. My father, Samuel, read and commented extensively upon this work in its various stages of manuscript evolution. I am likewise indebted to Greg Weller for years of friendship and, most important, for introducing me to King's fiction over a decade ago when he threw a copy of <u>Carrie</u> into my lap with the words "you must read this next." Michael Stanton and Norman Tederous both supplied me with insights to King's fiction that I never would have discovered personally. I would also be remiss if I failed to acknowledge Ted Dikty of Starmont House for his patience and steady encouragement as I sought extension after extension in the preparation of this manuscript. Finally, my greatest debt is to my students at the University of Vermont, particularly those who participated in English 261, fall term 1986, a senior seminar on the major work of Stephen King. Many of the ideas found between these covers originated in this seminar, and I wish to extend a special acknowledgement to the following individuals from that class whose imput was invaluable to the writing of this book: Leslie Day, Kristen Edwards, Laurie Girion, Steve Gorman, John Luter, and Leslie Paolucci.

Portions of this text were revised as a result of conference proceedings where work was initially aired to an academic audience. Parts of chapter two were presented at the 1987 International Conference on the Expressions of Evil in Literature and the Visual Arts, West Georgia College, Atlanta, while a modified version of chapter one was presented at the 1988 International Conference on the Fantastic in the Arts held in Fort Lauderdale, Florida. My thanks also to the Nathaniel Hawthorne Society and in particular John Idol, Jr., editor of the <u>Nathaniel Hawthorne Review</u>, for permitting me to re-employ the material of "Hawthorne's Woods Revisited: Stephen King's <u>Pet Sematary</u>," which appeared in the <u>Review</u>. A version of this chapter was likewise reprinted by Gary Hoppenstand and Ray Browne in their edited collection of critical essays entitled <u>The</u> <u>Gothic</u> <u>World</u> <u>of</u> <u>Stephen</u> <u>King:</u> <u>Landscape</u> <u>of</u> <u>Nightmares</u>, Bowling Green State University Popular Press, 1987.

                                                  Tony Magistrale
                                                  Burlington, Vermont
                                                  December 1987

Chapter 1
Moral Collapse:
Character, Setting, Free Will, and Tragic Designs

> . . . he looked to her like an absurd twentieth-century Hamlet, an indecisive figure so mesmerized by onrushing tragedy that he was helpless to divert its course or alter it in any way.
> --<u>The Shining</u>, 297

People read Stephen King's fiction for different reasons. In a recent issue of the local Burlington, Vermont newspaper, Erica Ruth Phillips, 17, Vermont's entry at the annual America's Junior Miss Pageant, a teenage version of the Miss America beauty contest, informed reporters that her two favorite books were <u>Uncle Tom's Cabin</u> and <u>Skeleton Crew</u>.

On an afternoon in July 1987, a man committed a grisly murder and evisceration in a hotel room outside of Pittsburgh, Pennsylvania. The word REDRUM was written several times on the walls of the room.

In Nevada, Missouri, a seventy-nine year-old grandmother told me that she buys Stephen King's books "the day they come out at our local bookstore . . . . I like his children the best; they remind me of my own babies, and they take me back long ago to when I was a child myself."

People read Stephen King's fiction for different reasons. Indeed, the selected evidence cited above merely suggests the wide range of his appeal and influence: from blue-eyed teenage beauty contestants, to sentimental grandmothers, to psychopathic criminals. His novels and story collections would not be responsible for making him America's most popular storyteller were he not speaking to readers on a variety of levels. The difficulty begins, however, when one tries to encapsulate, much less explain, the varied reasons for his success. For some, like Deborah Notkin and Donald Herron, the writer produces fiction that is simply good, exciting entertainment--a dark Disney, if you will. There is little debate, among those who have read even a couple of his short stories or one of his better novels, that the man can write. If you didn't mind the probability of not sleeping during the entire length of the night, Stephen King might be the type of person who would be a delightful companion on a camping trip: he tells a great tale. Anyone who has ever been forced to relinquish one of his books at the midway point of the narrative--even for a period of hours--appreciates the consummate skill of his ability to hold the reader hostage. And for many who purchase his books, this imaginative capacity is reason enough to admire his work.

Deborah Notkin argues in "Stephen King: Horror and Humanity for Our Time," that King has "achieved unprecedented popularity" because of his ability to produce escapist fiction: "Horror fantasy takes on an almost comforting aspect . . . [when] screaming newspaper headlines and graphic television news films bring every terrorist attack, border skirmish, technological near-disaster or other threat into our living room" (151-152). Similarly, Donald Herron in "The Biggest Horror Fan of Them All," feels that any attempt to analyze the "deeper meaning of going into a horror fun house" negates the fun of reading Stephen King (39). Herron firmly believes that "the majority of his fans or even his most intelligent critics" actually do not read King for complicated or serious reasons. And an attempt to do so, continues Herron, ultimately reduces the novel or story to the "dull drone . . . of another guy in a professor's hat" (38).

I will not use this opportunity to demean these positions, nor would I wish to: the great joy of good literature is within a response to the tale itself, and far be it for me or anyone to try and prescribe the manner in which the tale ought to be approached and enjoyed. But people read Stephen King for different reasons. I have always found his work to be <u>least</u> interesting when it descends into the merely grotesque or supernatural. Watching Carrie White single-handedly dismantle her town might have been great fun for Brian De Palma to direct, but the real dramatic energy of the text itself is gone by this point in the novel. Carrie White's familial torment and her struggles to belong to an adolescent peer group which will not make room for her are at the heart of <u>Carrie</u>, and watching her seek revenge on those who have so mercilessly tortured her into isolation is a little like watching a cornered child flailing at bullies who will not leave him alone: whatever dignity the child manages to summon, the observer must thereafter always assign a pathetic quality to his status.

I read Stephen King's fiction because I take it seriously. He has something to say about contemporary America, the people who are her citizens, and the deathless struggle to define morality, or what it costs to choose good over evil (and vice versa), which has been the subject of all great literature since the first tale was told at an evening campfire.

In her powerful essay entitled "The Fiction Writer and His Country," Flannery O'Connor justifies her use of violent and startling moments in fiction:

> The novelist with Christian concerns will find in modern life distortions which are repugnant to him, and his problem will be to make these appear as distortions to an audience which is used to seeing them as natural; and he may well be forced to take ever more violent means to get his vision across to this hostile audience. When you can assume that your audience holds the same beliefs you do, you can relax a little and use more normal means of talking to it; when you have to assume that it does not, then you have to make your vision apparent by shock--to the hard of hearing you shout, and for the almost-blind you draw large and startling pictures. (33-34)

King may not share O'Connor's fierce religious orientation, which is the catalyst that animates all of her marvelous tales of Southern life, but he certainly echoes her perspective on the need to resort to ever more violent and grotesque methods in order to retain an audience's attention. The horror story is the most appropriate genre for our time. After the devastation of Auschwitz and Hiroshima, the nuclear madness of missile diplomacy and "Star Wars" Strategic Defense Initiatives, the thrust of most traditional fiction is no longer capable of arousing or startling a modern audience "which is used to seeing [distortion and violence] as natural." The world of the nightmare, of monsters and sadistic and grotesque occurrences, speaks to us directly from the pages of daily newspapers and the videocameras of television newsrooms.

Ironically, in this age of science and rationalism, King's fiction maintains a level of cultural relevance that finds its closest historical parallel with the birth of Gothicism in the 1790's following the Age of Enlightenment. Just as Walpole's Castle of Otranto commenced the romantic rebellion against the deistic order of the eighteenth century, King's tales suggest two precepts that run counter to the fundamental premises of modern science: (1) that for every advance into the realm of chemistry and physics, there is a corresponding danger that that advance will produce a reaction beyond human control (e.g. nuclear energy and its by-product of highly radiocative fuel rods), and (2) that the universe is ultimately not a place open to human comprehension or domination.

In his imaginative and insightful book The Uses of Enchantment: The Meaning and Importance of Fairy Tales, Bruno Bettelheim theorizes that children require the mythos of the fairy tale because their level of cognitive development cannot accomodate the abstract realities of science and reason. Minds centered in "existing knowledge and emotional preoccupations" are overwhelmed by the vast complexities that measure and govern the world beyond the child's immediate consciousness. As he matures into the adult, however, the child's need for the magic traditionally associated with fairy tales and myths is displaced by the logic of reality and a personal identity that is not quite so fragile:

> For a long time in history man used emotional projections--such as gods--born of his immature hopes and anxieties to explain man, his society, and the universe; these explanations gave him a feeling of security. The slowly, by his own social, scientific, and

4

technological progress, man freed himself of the constant fear for his very existence. Feeling more secure in the world, and also within himself, man could now begin to question the validity of images he had used in the past as explanatory tools. (51)

When the meaning of the horror story is applied to Bettelheim's paradigm, we find a process at work that thrusts us back to childhood insecurities. It destroys the easy distinctions separating child and adult, erases the evolution by undercutting the means and reasons for personal and societal optimism. If "the fairy tale [must] proceed in a manner which conforms to the way a child thinks and experiences the world" (45), the horror story works in reverse--essentially subverting the manner in which adults prefer to apprehend the world by challenging the security of our faith in the very systems that currently sustain it. However, the point at which the horror story most closely approximates Bettelheim's conception of the fairy tale is in the mutual focus on "the dark sides of our personalities . . . . Children, not having their ids in conscious control, need stories which permit at least fantasy satisfaction of these 'bad' tendencies" (52). The horror story forces us to recognize the existence of evil in ourselves and in others; it shows us that although we may have managed to become adults, this fact does not necessarily mean we have learned how to behave.

The horror genre is thus a graphic reminder of human limitations and moral imperfections. Just as Flannery O'Connor felt the need to "make [her] vision apparent by shock," contemporary horror continues to hold up a mirror to our darkest personal urges and most repressive societal constraints. What the horror story shows us is that side of ourselves and our culture that we either find too uncomfortable to analyze to any great extent or continue to repress under the more complacent belief that we are well-intentioned beings for whom things inevitably work out. We want to believe that inherently all men are good. The tale of horror insists that they are not always good, and that the source of much that goes wrong in life is due to our own natures--the propensity of all men for acting violently, antisocially, selfishly, out of frustration and greed. Tim Underwood senses these very qualities about King's fiction when he writes in "The Skull Beneath the Skin" that

> In all of King's books, during moments of dreadful narrative intensity, reality, as we know of it, shifts. The safe world where terrible things do not happen to us dissolves and vanishes like the Emperor's new clothes-- as if our everyday vision of an amicable environment is merely a cloak which can be torn aside. (264)

In his essay "Imagery and the Third Eye" Stephen King dispenses some helpful advice to would-be writers regarding the importance of choosing language that is visual and detailed:

> . . . imagery does not occur on the writer's page; it occurs in the reader's mind. To describe everything is to supply a photograph in words; to indicate the points which seem the most vivid and important to you, the writer, is to allow the reader to flesh out your sketch into a portrait. (12)

King owes part of his enormous success as a writer of horror fiction to the fact that he consistently practices his own advice. We tend to accept the surreal events in his tales not so much because his monsters and creatures are so graphically rendered (although they are), but rather because they are introduced to a particular narrative after an appropriate build up of highly realistic situations. We are ready to acknowledge the existence of ghosts in The Shining because we have acknowledged the existence of the Torrance family. Consequently, as the Overlook's specters slowly begin to manifest themselves physically--first in the wasp's nest, then the animated hedge animals, the woman in room 217, and finally at the masquerade party--we readily accept their appearances. They do not occur until the novel is half over, when the reader is firmly ensconced within the isolated world of an autumn in Colorado with three members of a typical American family.

Moreover, King starts his gothic machinery slowly, commencing with simple wasps that refuse to die and concluding climatically with the unmasking of the entire hotel.

One of King's great fortes in this novel is his ability to hold the reader suspended for several chapters, blurred between the worlds of Jack's mind and the apparently objective events taking place inside the hotel. Only as the more credible testimonies of Danny and Wendy enter into the heart of the narrative are we convinced that Jack has not been merely hallucinating the Overlook's reawakening. King's ability, in other words, to render imaginary phenomena through realistic prose helps to create an atmosphere of confusion for the reader: Are we seeing things only through Jack's unstable psyche, or has the surreal become real? Are the Overlook's topiary hedge animals actually capable of locomotion, or is Jack suffering from a hallucination related to his withdrawal from alcohol and seculsion in the mountains? Indeed, it is not until Wendy herself witnesses and is included in the hotel's superanimation (Chapter 36, "The Elevator") that we become convinced the Overlook is actually haunted. And this conclusion, in and of itself, is a tremendous literary achievement--for outside the perimeters of The Shining, how many of us are willing to accept seriously the premise of a haunted hotel?

Ben P. Indick argues in "What Makes Him So Scary?", that "If a story of fear is to succeed, the characters and situations must be such as offer ready association for the reader; the dangers must be of a vitally important and basic nature, whether to the ego or to life itself" (9). This is an important tenet that I fully accept about King's fiction, and it at least partially explains why his work deserves to be taken so seriously. The themes representing the crux of his major novels are issues that bear immediate relevance to contemporary American life: the restrictive social world of American high schools (Carrie, Christine, "Sometimes They Come Back," and The Body); the moral corruption of small town America ('Salem's Lot and It); the dangerous intrusion of governmental manipulation of individual lives and the earth's chemistry (The

Stand, "Beachworld," "I am the Doorway," Firestarter, The Mist, The Dead Zone, and Roadwork); and the breakdown and breakup of the traditional American nuclear family (The Shining, "The Boogeyman," and Cujo). Obviously, the horrors in King's world are not restricted to the grotesque creatures and goblins of adolescent nightmares; they are also the stuff of which adult bad dreams are made.

In a recent interview in Fantasy Review, horror writer Robert R. McCammon argued persuasively for an understanding of the horror genre that includes a seriousness of purpose traditionally associated with "high art":

> Horror writing has always seemed to me a very liberal, forward-thinking kind of literature that is not afraid to shake things up. It's not afraid to be nasty. It's not afraid. And isn't that what art is all about?
> . . . Horror writers are approaching "real" horror, but we're doing it in such a way that is, hopefully, artistic and civilized. And in an educated and thoughtful way. We're not glorifying madness or murder or child abuse or any other of our twentieth-century horrors. We're simply trying to make sense out of the chaos, and in the process, explore ourselves as well. We have to go all the way in, to conduct exploratory surgery. And some surgery is done with a laser, and some with a saw. We may not like what we find, but we still have to know what's there. (24)

Leslie Fiedler has reminded us in books as diverse as Love and Death in the American Novel and Freaks that the popular literature of an era is an important vehicle for understanding the values and culture of its time. Studying the plethora of pornographic narratives that were so popular during the Victorian era, for example, reveals important insights into the tensions and anxieties of the English middle class. In other words, if a scholar wishes to comprehend the full dimensionality of a particular culture's historical time and place, he conceivably stands to learn as much from that era's popular literature as from studying its "mainstream" writers. Pauline Kael makes this point succinctly when she argues that

> pulp fiction, with its five-and-dime myths, can take a stronger hold on people's imagination than art because it doesn't affect the conscious imagination the way a great novel does, but the private, hidden imagination, the primitive fantasy life--with an immediacy that leaves no room for thought. (Underwood, 255)

Certainly Stephen King's fiction would appear to corraborate this thesis; the level of his popularity and the "hidden" relevancy of his texts insist that we consider his work, at least on one level of appreciation, as a social barometer of life in contemporary America.

In "Imagery and the Third Eye," King concludes his advice to writers by asking them to "take two pledges: First, not to insult your reader's interior vision; and second, to see everything before you write it" (14). Elsewhere in this same essay King suggests to his audience that the closest parallel to effective writing is a film camera that transports the viewer into the detailed imagery of a celluloid world.

In King's own fiction, the reader always shares in the knowledge of knowing exactly where she is. Even in the cross-country journeys that comprise whole sections of The Stand and The Talisman, we feel ourselves on the highway with the struggling protagonists. The lonely stretches of interstate asphalt, the dust of local dirt roads, even the sense of weariness that would attend such a trek are rendered with camera-like precision. King is a painter of landscapes and the dramatic moments of human struggle; his best fiction is focused and concrete--it defines settings which, even when they are not real and exist only in the realm of fantasy, are described with sufficient visual attention that the reader sees them with absolute clarity.

Several of King's novels and short stories are set in his native state of Maine. The use of Maine geography and personalities helps to maintain the high visual quality of King's fiction. He is writing about places and people he has known all his life, so that the task of "seeing everything before you write it" becomes all the more plausible and easier to produce. King's Maine is a place of definite textures and affiliations.

Burton Hatlen, himself a Mainer, perhaps comprehends and appreciates the regional influence on King's work better than any other critic. The "myth of Maine" that is gradually unfolding in King's fictional canon is a dark reflection of the state itself:

> And Stephen King too knows that there's something chillingly inhuman waiting out in those woods, hiding in the summer maybe, but as soon as the leaves begin to turn it crawls out, and someday when you're out jogging along a back road, or even just riding alone in your car, it stops and puts a cold finger right on your heart. (48)

In <u>Pet Sematary</u> Louis Creed's first journey beyond the Pet Sematary and into the burial grounds of the Micmac Indians occurs late in November. The absolute sense of an early New England winter, of an environment that is foreign to human habitation and survival, is developed with great success. Moreover, aside from capturing the raw flavor of Thanksgiving in the northeast (an experience that remains as distant to the consciousness of a Southerner or West Coast dweller as barbecued turkey is for an inhabitant of Maine), King's description of a cold and dismal landscape corresponds perfectly with Louis Creed's journey to a site that remains in active opposition to his best intentions and personal needs. As Louis makes his way past the deadfall and into the malevolent realm of the ancient Wendigo, a fierce combination of wind and cold assault him. Certainly the Maine geography and climate of this particular moment is meant to highlight the fact that the Wendigo is as much at home in this misanthropic surrounding as Louis Creed is not:

> The wind was sharper, colder, quickly numbing his face. <u>Are we above the treeline</u>?

he wondered. He looked up and saw a billion stars, cold lights in the darkness. Never in his life had the stars made him feel so completely small, infinitesimal, without meaning. He asked himself the old question--<u>is there anything intelligent out there</u>?--and instead of wonder, the thought brought a horrid cold feeling, as if he had asked himself what it might be like to eat a handful of squirming bugs. (114)

King's characters seldom feel a sense of pastoral harmony with the Maine landscape. His novels are not romantic postcard descriptions of a vacationland in the woods. Quite the opposite. The rural atmosphere of Maine is frequently a hostile and savage place composed of forces indifferent to human welfare as well as an environment where malefic supernatural energies reside (e.g. the Wendigo in <u>Pet Sematary</u>, the flying reptiles in <u>The Mist</u>, the deep winter woods that hide vampires in "Jerusalem's Lot," and the madness of a St. Bernard in <u>Cujo</u>). In <u>Pet Sematary</u> the land itself stands in opposition to the mortal will. The Micmac burial ground mocks Creed with its resurrected parodies of beings the doctor once loved; indeed, as if to measure the landscape's scorn for his efforts, even the doctor's attempt to cut into the Micmac soil in order to fashion a grave for his daughter's dead cat is met with extreme difficulty:

> The ground was stony and hard, and very quickly he saw that he was going to need the pick to dig the grave deep enough to hold Church . . . . Sometimes the pick would strike a rock hard enough to flash sparks, and the shiver would travel up the wooden shaft to vibrate in his hands. (116)

King's Maine is also a locale with distinct human personalities and dialects. While the writer is often critical of the state's small town communities and their attendant institutions (the high school in <u>Carrie</u>, the socially sanctioned levels of violence and racism in <u>It</u>, child abuse in <u>The Body</u>), <u>individual</u> Maine men and women are often placed in positions where they must rise above their unassuming and often oppressive origins in order to engage heroic action. Although King's Maine natives do not hold exclusive rights to moral perfection in his fiction, the majority share at least a general sense of human decency, treating others with acceptance and respect. Characters such as Ben Mears (<u>'Salem's Lot</u>), The Losers' Club (<u>It</u>), Johnny Smith (<u>The Dead Zone</u>), Frannie Goldsmith (<u>The Stand</u>), and Jud Crandall (<u>Pet Sematary</u>) are average men and women who are tested by above-average circumstances. Their unwillingness to relinquish their confidence in their own self-worth and secure identities, help them to overcome the unique moral challenges each encounters. Their rural and small town backgrounds have helped prepare these individuals to accept their struggles. Appropriate to their degree of self-confidence, most of these protagonists have no need for ostentatious behavior; there remains a quiet dignity (often bordering on stubbornness) that appears to be as much a characteristic of the New England personality as the simple acceptance of a harsh winter climate.

Johnny Smith, for example, possesses a tremendous paranormal insight that allows him to envision the future. Instead of exploiting this attribute for his own advantage, however, Smith applies his powers for the benefit of others--saving a group of young men and women by warning them of an imminent fire at a local restaurant, helping the police to capture a murder-rapist, and exposing the true personality of presidential candidate Greg Stillson.

When Smith emerges from his lengthy coma, he makes no attempt to intrude upon Sarah Bracknell, the woman he was scheduled to marry before his tragic car accident. And although he quietly withdraws from any selfish desire to complicate her life, he does not withdraw from life itself. There is a certain quality of Yankee stoicism to Smith's personality that links him to King's other Maine heroes and heroines; like them, he is a man of few words, but at the same time he is also fiercely independent, in possession of an intrinsic and uncomplicated moral code that remains consistent in the face of his personal tragedies.

King's generally positive attitude toward the inhabitants of his native state, however, must always be qualified. Burton Hatlen recognizes "a powerful ambivalence toward Maine" running through all of King's novels (50). King seems to understand intuitively that just as the Maine environment is capable of producing heroic individuals, it is also a place equally capable of destroying others because of its acute degree of isolation, pressure to conform, and small town narrowmindedness. As Hatlen concludes, "how many writers before King have so clearly delineated the hard, self-destructive streak that we find in so many Maine people? Edwin Arlington Robinson maybe--but I can't think of anyone else" (57).

In *'Salem's Lot* and *It*, for example, entire Maine communities are revealed to be highly susceptible to evil's dominion. Like the history of the Overlook Hotel, these two Maine towns attract and engender corruption. Their pasts share similar elements of human cruelty and infamous behavior on a grand scale; the evil that dominates Derry and Jerusalem's Lot resides within the individual community members, but also appears to be the natural consequence or inheritance of citizenship within either town. In 'Salem's Lot the level of corruption is so complete that only the cleansing action of an enormous bonfire (literally, the "good fire") is capable of restricting the vampire's advance from moving beyond the town limits.

Harold Lauder (*The Stand*), Joe Chamber (*Cujo*), Frank Dodd (*The Dead Zone*), and Mrs. Carmody (*The Mist*) are products of Maine's darker side. Devoid of any genuine compassion for the suffering that surrounds them, these characters appear to share much in common with the cruel and callous elements King affiliates with Maine's unsympathetic natural geography and climate. Like many of the winters he describes in such lurid detail, the aforementioned individuals apportioned no love for the human world. And just as the Maine environment is responsible for a state suicide rate (largely the consequence of the phenomenon known as "cabin fever") that remains the highest in America, these natives retreat into the self-destruction that attends human isolation. As such, they doom themselves in the void of a moral and ethical confusion. Their repudiation of humankind is highlighted through the mechanical imagery King associates with each of them--from the motorcycle that eventually seals Harold Lauder's annihilation on a bleak mountainside to Frank Dodd's fetishistic patterns of violation and murder.

  Much of the fiction in the horror genre is didactic, as the work of early American authors like Poe and Hawthorne attests, and with his own brand of horror, King continues to advance the tradition. The nineteenth-century American gothic tradition, to which King acknowledges an affiliation throughout Danse Macabre, used the gothic as a vehicle for testing and illustrating the Christian tenets of sin and redemption. The dramatization of these concepts required placing characters in situations in which they had the freedom to choose between degrees of evil and good.

  In King's novels, the concept of evil is rooted in both the individual himself (another influence of his New England heritage, as King fully subscribes to a Puritan sense of the pervasiveness of evil in the world), and the social community that surrounds him. Individuals in his fiction who succumb to the temptations of evil usually do so of their own volition. But King also acknowledges the existence of outside forces--particularly a malefic fate--that often bears some responsibility for the victimization of an individual. Keeping these distinctions in mind, King's view of human nature becomes more complex: while believing that human nature is certainly capable of surrendering itself freely to evil, he also determines that the tremendous pressure excited by foreign (or outside) malevolent agencies often compels mortals to commit acts that lead to self-destruction.

  In Danse Macabre King defines this bifurcated perspective: "All tales of horror can be divided into two groups: those in which the horror results from an act of free and conscious will--a conscious decision to do evil--and those in which the horror is predestinate, coming from outside like a stroke of lightning" (71). In what King goes on to distinguish as the tale of "psychological horror," certainly the most important contribution of the gothic genre, evil is the consequence of an individual's own lapse in moral judgment. Implicit in this perspective is the belief that what causes a person to choose evil is the presence of a personal flaw. The inheritance of Original Sin, which taints the entire human race, continually manifests itself in characters throughout gothic fiction. For example, as King cites in Danse Macabre, Frankenstein is the story of a man "creating a living being out of spare parts to satisfy his own hubris, and then compounding his sin by refusing to take responsibility for what he has done" (71-72). The source of evil in the story of Frankenstein, the reason Dr. Frankenstein chooses to fool with forces he should shun, is his over-developed ego.

Similar morally flawed characters exist in King's canon, and their shortcomings inevitably lead to the choice of performing evil over good. But as King himself has posited in his theory of "predestinate horror," many of these characters are likewise influenced, even manipulated toward self-annihilation through contact with outside forces and pressures that are capable of exploiting already existing human weaknesses.

Jack Torrance in The Shining is the clearest example of just such a character. He is a frustrated writer who has taken a job as caretaker of a hotel in Colorado with the hope that some peace and quiet away from the regular world, in which he has recently known nothing but bad luck, will supply him with the energy necessary to finish his play. But Jack's bad luck continues; he is never quite capable of pursuing his own best interests. Torrance is shaped by a personal history that is as destructive as that which he finds encapsulated within the Overlook's scrapbook (Chapter 18). Throughout the novel King carefully establishes parallels between Jack and his father: their common problem with alcohol, their tendencies toward violence, their abrupt tempers, and their shared love/hate relationships with their respective families. Most of all, however, Jack and his father are haunted by feelings of personal inadequacy. As Jack acknowledges to himself after his humiliating telephone conversation with Al Shockley: "How many times, over the years, had he--a grown man--asked for the mercy of another chance? He was suddenly so sick of himself, so revolted, that he could have groaned aloud" (184).

It is not merely Jack's association with an abusive father that locks him into a tragic design, however, for the Overlook itself is apparently capable of exerting its influence miles beyond the hotel's grounds. Al Shockley's nefarious connection as majority owner of the hotel, coupled with the events from Torrance's immediate past at Stovington that make Jack's employment as caretaker absolutely necessary, suggest the far-ranging methods available to the hotel for carrying out its purposes.

Early in the novel, before Jack has even set foot inside the Overlook's lobby, we learn of his decision to give up alcohol after a particularly frightening early-morning experience in Al's car. Driving together after a night of steady drinking, the car hits a riderless bicycle. And after the search for a body produces only the crumpled frame of the bicycle itself, "Jack thought later that some queer providence, bent on giving them both a last chance, had kept the cops away, had kept any of the passersby from calling them . . . [had placed a bicycle with] nobody riding it in the middle of the road" (39). Jack Torrance interprets the event optimistically, as the work of a divine authority benevolently disposed toward his welfare. But it is just as possible that the providence that put this bicycle in the middle of Jack's life is the same energy that conveniently placed the scrapbook of the Overlook's sordid history in a place next to the boiler where Jack was certain to find it. In the accident with the bicycle, this same providence might have anticipated that Jack and Al would be so frightened by the event that they would each give up alcohol completely--producing, of course, a tremendous psychological strain and susceptibility in Torrance that would culminate six months later in a full mental breakdown and a reintroduction to gin in the Colorado Lounge of the Overlook Hotel:

"Drink your drink, Mr. Torrance," Lloyd said softly. "It isn't a matter that concerns you.

Not at this point."
He picked his drink up again, raised it to his lips, and hesitated. He heard the hard, horrible snap as Danny's arm broke. He saw the bicycle flying brokenly up over the hood of Al's car, starring the windshield.
"Drink your drink," they all echoed.
He picked it up with a badly trembling hand. It was raw gin. He looked into it, and looking was like drowning. (343)

Once inside the Overlook, "like microbes trapped in the intestine of a monster" (211), the "management" of the hotel slowly creates a steady erosion of Jack's identity. In the methodical corruption of Torrance, the hotel exploits the most vulnerable aspects of his personality: his urge to sacrifice anything, including his family, for the success of his career; his unresolved tensions as a former alcoholic; the omnipresent undercurrent of marital discord and jealousy between Wendy and Jack that has threatened to culminate in divorce; and his ambivalent attitude toward the responsibilities of parenthood. Jack is victimized by the powers at the Overlook because from the very moment of his arrival he shares so much in common with it: "He promised himself he would take care of the place, very good care. It seemed that before today he had never really understood the breadth of his responsibility to the Overlook. It was almost like having a responsibility to history" (159).

There is a predestinate design at work at the Overlook, and it is in part responsible for Jack's mental and moral collapse. But it is a much too simplistic reading of this highly complex psychological horror story to assume that Jack's victimization is <u>only</u> the result of a deterministic fate over which he can exert no control.

After calling Ullman on the telephone, Jack vividly recalls a remark that Wendy had made several months earlier:

Once, during the drinking phase, Wendy had accused him of desiring his own destruction but not possessing the necessary moral fiber to support a full-blown deathwish. So he manufactured ways in which other people could do it, lopping a piece at a time off himself and their family. Could it be true? Was he afraid somewhere inside that the Overlook might be just what he needed to finish his play and generally collect up his shit and get it together? Was he blowing the whistle on himself? Please God no, don't let it be that way. Please. (182)

Throughout the novel we are presented evidence of Jack's ability to find excuses to rationalize his life's failures. As the above quote indicates, he feels out of control of his own life, or worse, secretly involved in his own self-destruction. In King's world, either of these positions brings the same result.

When stung by wasps early in the novel, Torrance views the moment in metaphorical terms: a man can no more anticipate moments of bad fortune in his life anymore than he can remain in control of himself while being stung by angry wasps: "Could you be expected to live in the love of your nearest and dearest when the brown, furious cloud rose out of the hole in the fabric of things (the fabric you thought was so innocent) and arrowed straight at you" (110)? Here Torrance raises a persuasive argument for the existence of a deterministic universe--a place where an individual is always at the mercy of Fortune's capricious will. And while we have already spoken of the Overlook's capabilities to shape the circumstances of Fate to its own ends, it is also clear that Danny, Wendy, and Hallorann are able to circumvent its design. Why does Jack fall prey to "the wasp nest of life" while these others manage to endure and even surmount the trap that is set at the Overlook? The difference appears to lie in Jack's self-pitying posture. Although he hopes that Wendy's judgment on his self-destructive impulses is incorrect, the fact that he remains tentative about this judgment throughout the novel leaves him without the confidence, loyalty, or self-discipline that the others employ in their successful battle against the perverse powers at the Overlook: ". . . he was the vulnerable one, the one who could be bent and twisted until something snapped" (279).

Jack willingly surrenders what remains of his own freedom at several critical points in the narrative. He <u>decides</u> not to look at what is inside the bath tub in room 217; he <u>decides</u> not to flee the hotel in the snowmobile, and likewise makes it impossible for Wendy and Danny to leave; he <u>chooses</u> not to act on the feelings of self-preservation and the love he possesses for his son; and he makes a deliberate decision to release the pressure in the boiler, even as the voice in his head cries "<u>Go get Wendy and Danny and get the fuck out of here. Let it blow sky-high</u>" (326). We become fully cognizant of Jack's wasted freedom and his forfeited potential to change the course of events at the Overlook in his final confrontation with Danny on the third floor of the hotel. Even at this late stage in the hotel's vampirism of Jack's identity, when Torrance appears to be most completely absorbed in the service of the Overlook, some part of his mind is able to respond to the love he once shared with his son, forcing the Jack-creature to drop the deadly mallet and allow Danny to escape:

> The face in front of him changed. It was hard to say how; there was no melting or merging of the features. The body trembled slightly, and then the bloody hands opened like broken claws. The mallet fell from them and thumped to the rug. That was all. But suddenly his daddy was there, looking at him in mortal agony, and a sorrow so great that Danny's heart flamed within his chest . . . .
> "Doc," Jack Torrance said. "Run away. Quick. And remember how much I love you." (428)

<u>The Shining</u> tells a story of one man's manipulation by a malefic fate and the remembrances of things past which continue to haunt his present. But in the end, the final decisions that result in Jack's affiliation with either moral extreme are always his to make. Indeed, the Overlook can only <u>shape</u> the circumstances of Jack's life; he is given final control over how they are to be interpreted. And

on each occasion in the novel the consequences of his action (or non-action) make him personally responsible for the tragedy that ensues. Through out the way to his ruin, Torrance appears to be fully conscious of the Overlook's ultimate intentions: "If you play the game with us, we'll play the game with you. Position of responsibility. They wanted him to sacrifice his son" (352). Unwilling to say no to the game, unable to summon the courage necessary to distinguish good from evil, the family of man from a family of ghouls, Jack perishes as he has chosen to live--as a man without an identity of his own: "Then the mallet began to rise and descend, destroying the last of Jack Torrance's image.... What remained of the face became a strange, shifting composite, many faces mixed imperfectly into one" (429).

While it is true that the Overlook's authority extends beyond the hotel itself--as I have suggested, perhaps even beyond Colorado--it is also true that its will is not omnipotent. Indeed, King asserts, especially through Hallorann's character, that the will of evil is not indomitable and that human choices of moral action can ultimately thwart whatever design evil composes. In contrast to Jack's capitulation, Hallorann's personal discipline and moral commitment to the welfare of others enables him to reject both the Overlook's command that he "GET OUT OF HERE . . . THIS IS NONE OF YOUR BUSINESS" (389), and its final attempt to seduce him into serving its violent will (439). Unlike Jack, Hallorann serves as an excellent example of the terrible freedom that is the responsibility King's characters must carry: the choice to resist the lure of evil belongs to the individual. The circumstances of fate may work to facilitate evil's animation, but man alone, as Danny Torrance also illustrates, ultimately controls the key to his own destiny.

The final pages of <u>The Shining</u> summarize the novel's treatment of the interplay of individual free will and the determinism of fate. Hallorann's response to Danny's loss of his father reflects the co-existence of both these positions. He begins by informing the boy that "The world's a hard place, Danny. It don't care. It don't hate you and me, but it don't love us either. Terrible things happen in the world, and they're things no one can explain" (446). Essentially, Hallorann is here acknowledging the callous mechanism of fate; as we have seen, the Torrance family has witnessed first-hand just how hard a place the world can be in their experience at the Overlook. The force that animated the hotel possessed cosmic energy on a scale beyond the mortal realm. And while the shine appears as an effective counterbalance to this energy, Wendy and Danny endure only because of their own <u>human</u> resourcefulness and the moral courage of a black chef. There is no God available to intercede directly on their behalf, no Supreme Force of Good to make the "terrible things" retreat back into the shadows or to explain away Danny's pain; the only avenue for salvation in Stephen King's universe is through the faith and loyalty that human beings share with each other.

And the full implications of this last point are exactly what motivates Hallorann in the remainder of his conversation: "'See that you get on. That's your job in this hard world, to keep your love alive and see that you get on, no matter what'" (446). Although fate, like the Overlook itself, remains indifferent to human welfare, Hallorann reminds Danny of a truth that Jack Torrance never fully comprehended. The individual possesses the ability--if he "keeps his love alive"--to endure the ravages of fate. Although we may all be cosmic orphans, stung frequently by the inhabitants of Jack's "wasp nest of life," we still have each other, as the union among Danny, Hallorann, and Wendy is meant to exemplify. Hallorann dramatizes a secular faith that is similar to the existential credo that informs the work of Albert Camus: while we are all ultimately alone in this "hard place," as long as we remain here together we have a moral responsibility to help one another "'to get on, no matter what.'"

Perhaps Hallorann's purpose in alerting Danny to these facts is to insure that the boy does not follow in the footsteps of his father and grandfather. It is not beyond plausible speculation that Danny, the powers of the shining notwithstanding, could someday become convinced, especially in light of his gruesome experiences at the Overlook, that he has been unfairly victimized in a world "that don't love us." Hallorann feels the need to balance this deterministic reality with a reminder of the freedom and its attendant responsibilities that human beings nonetheless possess. Jack Torrance never fully established this balance, either in theory or in practice. Rather, he abandoned himself to self-pity and sacrificed in the process whatever opportunity remained to deepen his capacities for love and survival. Hallorann wants Danny to struggle against a similar capitulation, for the black man knows that the child will face a struggle--Danny's own personal history now shares too many parallels with Jack's.

Jack Torrance's tragic example is the consequence of a moral collapse that is the result of personal liabilities aiding the malevolent design of a predestinate evil. Arnie Cunningham's situation in <u>Christine</u> is curiously similar. Although Arnie does not become an active agent of evil, as Jack does in <u>The Shining</u>, he does exhibit an unwillingness to choose good over evil in his refusal to destroy the car that he is almost certain has killed several people. Whereas Torrance is motivated by an unsatisfied quest for fame and fortune (he is certain that the hotel must want him more than it wants Danny), Arnie suffers analogous feelings of inadequacy and frustration:

> He was a loser, you know. Every high school has to have at least two; it's like a national law . . . . Everyone's dumping ground . . . [he] was a natural out. He was out with the jocks . . . out with the high school intellectuals . . . out with the druggies ... out with the macho pegged-jeans-and-Lucky-Strikes group . . . and he was out with the girls. (1)

Cunningham becomes obsessed with his new car because it offers him the self-esteem that the social hierarchy of his high school denies him. As Dennis points out, losers like Arnie need to "find something to hang onto . . . . And [Arnie] had Christine" (495). But in his initial purchase of the car, Arnie does not make a conscious choice between good and evil. In fact, it is the car that has chosen Arnie, just as the Overlook appears to have ordained Jack's arrival as caretaker.

Arnie's choice only comes later, after he has the strong suspicion that Christine has a life of her own and has been carrying out a pattern of revenge against the people who have tormented him. Arnie can choose, at this point, to abandon the car, but in doing so he knows he would also be forced to relinquish the new levels of self-esteem and social confidence Christine has engendered. Like Jack, who consciously sacrifices his family for the sake of his caretaker "responsibilities," Arnie chooses to ignore the fact that Christine is an agent for Le Bay's corruption.

The issue here, as in the case of Torrance, is who or what is ultimately responsible for Arnie's destruction? His highly personal susceptibilities certainly make him an easy mark for Christine's flashy charms and the promise of a new life in a world where he is accepted. Forced into the role of a loser, with all the stigmas attached to that distinction, Arnie is frightened of losing the power he has so recently gained. This legitimate fear is what keeps him from giving up the car. Certainly what sets Arnie up for his fall is the rigid social caste system that dominates life in his high school. As with Torrance, Arnie's tragedy is the result of his own inability to measure his desire for success and identity against the moral cost he must eventually pay.

In interviews and in several places throughout <u>Danse Macabre</u> King tells us that the most important task a fiction writer must accomplish--particularly a writer of fantasy--is the development of character to the point at which a reader comes to care about the fate of a protagonist. King not only makes us painfully aware of the unique individuals and the particular problems they must confront in his fiction, but he also forces us to respond to them. We feel pity and terror for Arnie Cunningham and Jack Torrance as they lose control over themselves. We feel tremendous sympathy for Carrie White's humiliation at the hands of her less generous peers; we worry about Jack Sawyer as his quest takes him further from his childhood.

What we cannot do is to dismiss these people; we must care about their histories and fates. As Thomas Monteleone suggests, "If you take away the interesting, well-drawn characters in King's novels and stories, you have some pretty ordinary tales" (241). As the reader becomes more involved in the moral and physical struggles of King's protagonists, she both escapes from her world for a little while, and yet also sees that same world projected back at her with startling revelations. This is King's great skill: the ability to place the reader in an imaginative realm of supernatural events that still manage to convey something of critical significance, even if it is disguised through metaphor or allegory, about the actual everyday realm she inhabits. Don Herron argues in "Horror Springs in the Fiction of Stephen King" that "[King] has done some things supernaturalists have not done before. His characters swear. They excrete. They often act crudely, grossly" (89). I suspect the reasons for King's enormous popularity reach far beyond these fundamental physical acts. The full implications of Herron's remark, however, do suggest a reader's identification with the everyday aspects of his fiction: his characters are real. The actions and problems they encounter are real. None of his fictional men and women enters our lives without exacting some kind of response. King's best fiction is an illustration of the mystique that compels us to read literature at all--to laugh, to feel, to share in the high terror of tragedy and the exultation of survival.

Part One: When Good and Evil Collide

> We fall from womb to tomb, from one blackness and toward another, remembering little of one and knowing nothing of the other . . . except through faith.
> --<u>Danse Macabre</u>, 380

The shape evil takes in Stephen King's fiction is as varied as the creatures that populate it. Sometimes it resides in an inhuman object or edifice predisposed toward violent animation. The Overlook Hotel, Christine, and the Marsten House in <u>'Salem's Lot</u>, for example, are entry points for evil's intrusion into the mortal world. However, it is also apparent that the evil assembled in these places would not be capable of exerting such an active presence over human affairs without first gaining its strength and influence from earlier moments of human misconduct. The Overlook's current power comes from an elaborate history of murder or mayhem enacted within its walls. Similarly, Count Barlow chooses the Marsten House quite deliberately: the murder/suicide of its previous owners make it receptive to a vampire's pursuits. As the first chapter's discussion of free will posits, to manifest its authority evil always requires a human agent to make a deliberate choice in the rejection of good. In <u>It</u> the stellar nucleus for Pennywise remains dormant outside of Derry until the town's first human inhabitants arrive to supply it with life. As the Losers' Club uncovers in the Smoke-Hole ceremony, evil in King's universe is omnipresent; it appears in a context closely resembling the concept of original sin. But human choice also seems capable of dictating the degree of influence associated with evil's design. King accepts the premise that the mortal world has inherited the taint of Adam and Eve's initial transgression, but he likewise believes that evil cannot gain ultimate triumph unless the individual so wills it. In practically every Stephen King tale good and evil are given body in the form of some figures and their actions, as good and evil are omnipresent in life and the propensities for both are present in all of us. It is this duality which poses the moral problem, and requires a courageous struggle against what seem like overwhelming odds to solve it. As is the condition in Hawthorne's tales and sketches, a malefic spirit dominates King's landscapes, casting a shadow that obscures the divine presence. But what is available after the darkness of birth and tomb are recognized, is the persistence of faith. King's faith in the endurance of a traditional morality, based on the values of love and the resiliency of the human spirit, power whatever light remains in a world actively pursuing the destruction of itself and everything within it. Evil revels in our isolation from one another, but when the dark force fails to establish this isolation, it crumbles in the light of our own human liberation. This is the truth Dick Hallorann has discovered in his winter trek to the Overlook. He receives help and comfort from every human being he encounters on his noble errand to save Danny and Wendy from the inhuman forces that threathen their lives. Indeed, without such living examples of faith and love, we must become like Jack Torrance and Louis Creed: mad voices crying in the dead of night.

Chapter 2
The Devil in the Machine:
Technological Boogeymen

"If a nuclear war starts, it's going to start by accident; it's not going to start because it's intended."
--Senator Joseph R. Biden, contender for the Democratic Presidential nomination, July 1, 1987

In an age where computers and high-tech equipment have provided man with advanced security devices for his home, automobile, and business, ironically his life has become no more secure. Threatened daily by nuclear annihilation, the dark sister of the technological family which made these advanced security systems possible, modern men and women must learn to function in an atmosphere of anxiety. Throughout the greater body of his fiction, Stephen King addresses the dual genies of science and technology gone bad-- the dim results of man's irresponsibility and subsequent loss of control over those things which he himself has created.

The anti-technological bias in King's work is certainly rooted in his awareness of the type of "accident" cited by Senator Biden. As King remarked to Douglas Winter in an interview published in <u>Faces</u> <u>of</u> <u>Fear</u>:

> The thing that I come back to since <u>The Stand</u> is that all of those things are laying around waiting for somebody to pick them up-- you know, the gadgetry. And I get haunted by the idea of gadgets, because that's all it is--gadgets. It's all stuff hooked together with rubber bands and Elmer's Glue; it's all insert Tab A into Tab B. And we <u>love</u> things like that . . . .
> So now we have nuclear bombs, we have stuff that can kill twenty million people in twelve seconds. CBW, nerve gas, the nukes, all of this stuff, it's just gadgets, that's all it is. Our technology has outraced our morality. And I don't think it's possible to stick the devil back in the box. I think it will kill us in the next twenty years.

> Every day, when I wake up and turn on the news, I wait for someone to say that Paris was obliterated last night . . . by a gadget. It's only the grace of God that has kept it from happening so far. (252-253)

King's frequent criticism of modern man's infatuation with lethal machinery extends beyond the threat of war to include the elements of depersonalization and social estrangement that are likewise products of the technological age. The threat in stories such as <u>Christine</u> or "The Mangler" is not only in the machines themselves, but also in the human vulnerability to dehumanization. In King's mind, the alienation of the assembly line has emerged from beyond the factory wall to become a living presence in the consumer's life. In the tales "Graveyard Shift" and "Sometimes They Come Back" it is quite impossible to separate the occurrence of supernatural phenomena from the existence of human alienation at the workplace. As a corollary to these levels of human depersonalization, machines are often personified in King's stories--invested with wills of their own--and as these inanimate objects come to life, the human world is correspondingly imperiled. It is interesting that so many of King's mechanical creations appear to be driven by some kind of force of moral retribution destined to punish humankind for its scientific "accidents" and moral transgressions. In the short tale "Uncle Otto's Truck," for example, an old pick-up truck is brought to life after it is used to help a businessman murder his partner.

In order to obtain a more detailed perspective on the role of technology in King's fiction, consider two of his most important narratives which develop this theme: "Trucks" and the novella <u>The Mist</u>. The structures and settings of both stories share physical as well as symbolic similarities. "Trucks" takes place in a greasy roadside diner inhabited by hungry truckers pulling off the nearby highway, while <u>The Mist</u> centers around a local foodstore, the Federal Foods Supermarket, on the day following a severe electrical storm. Both diner and supermarket represent typical American settings, common scenarios in modern life and fiction which are easily recognized and visualized by the reader. King sets up the calm before the real storm by placing his characters in ordinary environments that would normally appear to be secure and nonthreatening. A crucial element in both tales is the writer's ability to build on the latent but realistic fear that one day similar accidents might actually occur, and more than likely the reader would be eating a hamburger in a local diner or purchasing a quart of milk in the dairy section of the supermarket when they do.

These surroundings, and the characters who inhabit them, serve as a microcosm of the larger world. In this realistically inspired, albeit reduced view of society, King illustrates the havoc man has wreaked upon himself through his short-sighted inventions and blind scientific groping. The characters are at the mercy of their society's scientific creations. And always there exists the question of responsibility: who or what has allowed things to get to the point where the human world is no longer in control of its gadgets? In much of his fiction King posits the thesis that society has relinquished its moral responsibilities to an elite group of technocrats who, in turn, has abused and forfeited these responsibilities. In The Mist the group operates under the title "the Arrowhead Project," which refers to a mysterious government operation in rural Maine whose purpose and functions remain illusive and encourage curious speculations:

> That was old Bill Giosti's theory about the so-called Black Spring: the Arrowhead Project. In the western part of Shaymore, not far from where the town borders on Stoneham, there was a small government preserve surrounded with wire. There were sentries and closed-circuit television cameras and God knew what else. Or so I had heard; I'd never actually seen it, although the Old Shaymore Road runs along the eastern side of the government land for a mile or so . . . .
> "Atomic things," Bill said that day, leaning in the Scout's window and blowing a healthy draught of Pabst into my face.

> "That's what they're fooling around with up there. Shooting atoms into the air and all that." "Mr. Giosti, the air's full of atoms," Billy had said. "That's what Mrs. Neary says. Mrs. Neary says everything's full of atoms."
> Bill Giosti gave my son Bill a long, bloodshot glance that finally deflated him. "These are <u>different</u> atoms, son." (43)

Governmental misuse of authority in its pursuit of greater technological advances is a common theme in King's work. In <u>Firestarter</u>, The Shop, a clandestine agency secretly funded by the CIA, engages in unethical genetic experimentation that produces chromosome damage to Charlie McGee and her mother and father. In <u>The Stand</u> the implication is clear that a bureaucratic mistake is responsible for releasing the superflu that nearly annihilates humanity. In each of these instances the American government is directly culpable for perverse acts of intrusion into the lives of innocent citizens. Moreover, to protect itself and its technological secrets, this same government always employs unscrupulous activities to reduce its liabilities and cover-up its failings.

<u>Firestarter</u> is a novel about the misuse of power: the lengths The Shop will go in order to obtain control over the supernatural capabilities it has helped to engender within Charlie McGee. Rainbird's personal betrayal of Charlie serves as an appropriate metaphor for the larger betrayal of trust between the American government and the innocent citizens who are victimized by its aversion to the truth. In the eyes of the technocrats who operate The Shop, Charlie McGee's pyrokenetic ability, like the "Arrowhead Project" in <u>The Mist</u>, is nothing more than another technological gadget to be used and exploited for military purposes. To own the power affiliated with such weaponry, King's governmental organizations pursue any lengths, even at the expense of individual human lives.

The qualities of mystery and ambiguity, which remain associated with King's governmental operations throughout his fiction, serve to highlight the uncertain nature of the technology being advanced by these bureaucratic organizations. Although left with questions still unresolved at the end of each of the narratives mentioned in this chapter, they all share a common perspective: the guidelines for moral behavior were either aborted or abandoned in the governmental quest for greater technological expertise. In "Trucks" a blamable source is not readily apparent, but the same idea is inferred: somewhere, somebody's tests backfired. In the diner, the trucker wonders aloud: "'What would do it? . . . Electrical storms in the atmosphere? Nuclear testing?'" (130).

    Besides developing similar settings and themes, The Mist and "Trucks" share certain "stock" figures who possess similar personalities and characteristics. Most obvious are the two narrators--David Drayton in The Mist and the nameless speaker in "Trucks." They are the protagonists who operate in the roles of stabilizers throughout the crises, the voices of reason and rational thought who exert some balanced measure of control amidst the panic and near hysteria that are the consequences of each respective technological accident. These are the characters with the strongest commitment to human welfare and the greatest levels of clarity, whose judgment remains unimpaired in every instance, whether other individuals choose to listen or not.
    Also included in this comparison of similar characters within these two tales is the teenage boy, the blue collar tough guy, and the middle-aged male "disbeliever." Each figure functions basically the same way in both stories and experiences nearly identical fates.
    The two young teens in The Mist, displaying the reckless bravado of youth, are eager and willing to help in the search for a means of escaping or bettering their situations. But in their eagerness, both young men become the victims of the malevolent force from the outside. The trucker in "Trucks" and Jim and Myron (the flower) LaFleur in The Mist are King's traditional roughnecks who grasp for solutions and stubbornly cling to them at great expense, against the sage advice of the central narrators. In both

instances, this ends in disaster. After bodily threatening David for trying to interfere with the teen's decision to open the loading door, Myron and Jim are left humbled and guilty when a boy is killed, the victim of their poor judgment as much as the tentacled monster outside: "Jim looked down at his Dingo boots. Myron sat on the floor and held his beer belly . . . 'Let's get out of here,' Myron said. 'I'm sorry about the kid. But you got to understand--'" (76). In "Trucks" the truckdriver also disagrees with the narrator, deciding to wait and let the thirsty, grumbling trucks run out of gas, rather than capitulating to their will by filling the gas tanks. Before long, the narrator is proven the wiser, as a bulldozer begins smashing down the front walls of the diner.

A recurrent motif in King's fiction pursues the manner in which human beings pull back together in the aftermath of society's collapse. In both stories the characters trapped in the diner and grocery store unconsciously begin reorganizing themselves within the confines of their unstable worlds in an attempt to establish some control over their horrifying fates. The suggestion in both stories is that while the technological world is devoid of stability--capable, like Hitchcock's birds, of unleashing its misanthropic force at any time--within the human community there is the eternal promise of hope in our capacity for sympathy and love. Whatever power is responsible for producing the dual terrors of prehistoric beasts in The Mist and rampaging trucks in "Trucks," both the force itself and it malevolent manifestations are profoundly anti-human. In relinquishing our humanity to accomodate the demands of life in the technological age, we leave ourselves open to consequences that reflect our abandonment of morality. It is thus particularly unnerving when the narrator of "Trucks" looks up at an airplane overhead and hopes that there is a flesh and blood pilot inside. His fear, shared by the small community under seige in The Mist, is that the human world has been essentially displaced by the mechanical--that the technology we extol has produced a perverse energy that owes allegiance to no one.

"Trucks," written in 1973, is the basis for the original plot and character structure that later becomes The Mist. The people who are trapped in the diner are assembled against evil consequences of the technology outside. They automatically begin voting on group decisions and unconsciously gravitate towards the strongest leaders among them, falling back on remnants of past social behavior.

Written seven years later, The Mist is also reminiscent of the classic novel Lord of the Flies, and King's own The Stand, in their respective studies of human interaction and the evolution of social interdependencies which occur when human beings attempt to re-group after a destructive crisis. Like Lord of the Flies, factions begin to appear within the supermarket, separating the individuals on the basis of morality or religious beliefs. The "Flat Earthers" is the first group to break away and is led by David's neighbor, Brent Norton. The members who refuse to believe what is occurring decide to take their chances and journey out into the mist. The second, and more dangerous group, is led by Mrs. Carmody, the local religious fundamentalist and self-proclaimed psychic who works enough people into a frenzy with her zealotry to generate a sizable following. The third group are those people left in the supermarket who gravitate towards the gentle strength of David Drayton and Ollie Weeks, who try to maintain rational thought and behavior. As in The Stand, good faction is pitted against bad, and human morals are reduced to contemplation of murder and blood sacrifice.

This breakdown of contemporary society is most vividly apparent in King's constant references to a prehistoric age where dinosaur-like monsters come to life in the mist and are personified in the semi's and tractor-trailer trucks. Man is viewed as having created a technology that has gone beyond the realm of his control, and King addresses what happens when that technology betrays its creator. He suggests in both "Trucks" and The Mist that technology will eventually turn on the human world, enslaving it and reducing society to a primitive, dark age.

It is interesting that King defines the

horrors in each of these tales in specifically prehistoric imagery: flying reptiles resembling Pteranodons in The Mist and lumbering vehicles that are compared to hulking dinosaurs in "Trucks." His choice of describing technological misadventures through prehistoric consequences is deliberate, indicating that modern man's false sense of superiority to his prehistoric legacy is based exclusively on his technological achievements. By further analogy, in placing modern man in a prehistoric context after the breakdown of his technologies, King suggests similar vulnerabilities between the two eras of history: like their primitive ancestors, the modern characters in these tales find themselves not only isolated in their contemporary caves (the diner and supermarket) but involved likewise in a struggle in which their only weapons are once more their hands and mental resourcefulness. And yet unlike primitive man, who at least possessed a keen awareness of his environment, King's modern men and women are divorced from their respective world, abruptly assaulted by a radically mutated nature they have unwittingly helped to unleash. In short, primitive man was a part of his world; he had a place in it. Modern man, at least in King's eyes, is an alien in a foreign environment his technologies have helped to create and foster.

Faced with no choice but to submit to the giant, hulking creatures, the characters in "Trucks" begin feeding them, recoiling from the stench of gas, "The same stink that the dinosaurs must have died smelling as they went down into the tar pits" (141). King puts forth the image of the entire modern age sinking into the quagmire of a landscape betrayed by a misapprehended faith in technology, and perhaps vanishing like the dinosaurs, leaving the likes of those creatures in the mist to rule the earth. At the close of "Trucks" the narrator ponders man's ultimate fate against the humanized trucks: "We could run, maybe . . . through the marshy places where trucks would bog down like mastadons and go--back to the caves. Drawing pictures in charcoal . . . (142).

David Drayton's dream in The Mist is likewise reminiscent of the price man must pay for his over-reliance on technology:

> And then a bird rose out of the waterpout, a gigantic scarlet "oiseau de mort" whose prehistoric wingspan darkened the entire lake . . . and as it came to gobble up my wife and son, a low sinister voice began to whisper over and over again: The Arrowhead Project. (111)

The bird, technology's spawn, snuffs out the civilization man has been building for thousands of years on the foundation of ever-advancing levels of technological evolution.

King's switch from past tense to present tense in the last few pages of each story is an effective horror technique. Suddenly, and without warning, the reader is pulled into the narrator's terrifying world, aware that the nightmare is not over, and is indeed spreading as he reads these very words: "As I write this, it is a quarter to one in the morning . . . I am writing by the light of a big Delco flashlight . . . every now and then there is a louder thud as one of the birds takes off" (153). Both narrators have survived what we hope has been the worst. There are only a few paragraphs remaining in each tale, and yet in both instances there is no real conclusion. As the narrator of __The Mist__ addresses his audience in the midst of his experience, even "that great old standby: It was all a dream" remains unavailable (152). In "Trucks" King seems to have given up on human survival and doomed it to an eternity of slavery serving its own creatures. In terms of the horror potential, this is a terrifying conclusion, but it lacks the deeper insight and complexity of __The Mist__.

Perhaps the only glimmer of hope that appears in either of these technological nightmares is in the form of "one word" the narrator of __The Mist__ believes he has heard on a radio after escaping from the grocery store. The author seems to suggest that man might have a chance to rebuild, and perhaps this story ends where __The Stand__ begins--in the reconstruction and change that must take place after civilization's slate has been violently wiped clean. Both here and in __The Stand__ King is theorizing that human survival will be possible only after the technological demons have been allowed to run their course, leaving man to begin again from his primitive origins. As Stu Redman postulates at the conclusion of The Stand, there is always the possibility that this new man may yet learn from the mistakes of the old world, forming a new society based on human rather than technological values.

Together, The Mist and "Trucks" make a strong statement about the status of technology in modern American society. King takes the reader to a time and place that is certainly not beyond the imagination, where all human control is relinquished and man finds himself lost in a dark and primitive future of fear and retribution. Whether it be a mist full of gruesome reptiles, or trucks with minds of their own, King warns the coming of that black bird of death which bears as many names as it does feathers--from the Arrowhead Project, to Three Mile Island, to the Rhine River, to Chernobyl.

In both "Trucks" and The Mist the terror of the unknown contains a lethal threat for humanity. But each tale also describes a terror of equal proportions in the evil of man's inhumanity to man. In The Mist, David, his son, and the two women elect to embark on a journey away from the supermarket, the novella's microcosmic society. They choose to risk the malevolence of the reptiles rather than to remain within the inhospitable social milieu of the supermarket. King's implicit criticism of human society in The Stand, The Mist, and "Trucks" is an extension of the alienation theme that he associates with an advanced state of technology.

In The Stand, for instance, Glen Bateman suspects that Flagg is an attractive alternative for the reamining technocrats in America; Flagg's obsession with order and gadgetry would appeal to similar impulses within King's technocrats:

> "I think he's going to get most of the techies," Glen said finally. "Don't ask me why; it's just a hunch. Except that tech people like to work in an atmosphere of tight discipline and linear goals, for the most part. They like it when the trains run on time. What we've got in Boulder right now is

mass confusion, everyone bopping along doing his own thing . . . . (396)

Given King's bleak perspective on technology, it is hardly surprising that Las Vegas is a place of technological sophistication with a correspondingly high level of personal alienation, while Boulder maintains a level of interpersonal harmony so long as it remains technologically naive. King's indictment of the technological age thus expands beyond the gadgetry and machinery itself, to include the social relationships that bear the mark of technology's influence. Modern American society, in King's eyes, has become a mere reflection of the machine age: Sacrificing individual and collective moral codes for the sake of attaining greater levels of authority and material well-being, King's America is a virtual machine operating without a driver at the helm.

As the inanimate world obtains greater power in King's fiction, it does so at the expense of the human world's autonomy and control. The pattern often takes this shape: as man allows himself to become more dehumanized, more reliant on his technological hardware, inanimate objects--particularly machines--grow proportionately in stature, as if the supernatural force in control of these objects is inspired by and takes its strength from the moral void created within human capitulation. The Overlook exerts a correspondingly greater influence over the lives of the Torrance family as their familial union loses its cohesiveness and Jack relinquishes his humanity to become a permanent member of the hotel's staff. Christine's self-regenerative powers reach maximum capacity as Arnie Cunningham forfeits his own identity in order to become one with Roland Le Bay and his rolling coffin.

In related instances, many of the most morally deficient characters in King's canon have exchanged their morality for the dream of technological conquest. Flagg in The Stand, Morgan Sloat in The Talisman, even Greg Stillson in The Dead Zone employ technology to help them in their respective quests for worldly domination. For each of these men, the lethal gadgetry of the modern age is an endless fascination, a means either to cripple society to make conquest possible, or, should their wills be somehow thwarted, the final catastrophic solution to avoid acknowledging defeat. In either case, as a means to power or as a method to end it, technology--nuclear weaponry in particular--is used to serve the design of unscrupulous men of power; it is nothing less than a reflection of their own egos: if the world will not capitulate to their respective tyrannical visions, then the world will simply cease to exist. Like King Sardanapalus, who, out of a supreme egocentrism, chose to watch all of the living beings who had ever provided him with pleasure sacrificed in front of him before his own death, Flagg, Stillson, and Sloat would each give the command to end civilization for the mere pleasure of watching his order fulfilled.

Morgan Sloat is one of the great villains in Stephen King's fiction. Not only does Sloat murder his business partner and best friend, Jack Sawyer's father, but he continues to torment Jack and his dying mother as they try to escape him across the country. But Sloat's greatest act of infamy in a lifetime of vile perpetrations is his attempt, and partial success, in despoiling the Territories through the introduction of nuclear weapons. Throughout The Talisman the Territories represent a neo-Eden, contrasting sharply with the polluted and debased landscape of contemporary America. Jack's hairy friend, Wolf, is a barometer of the differences between the two environments as he is unable to remain in America for great lengths of time since its air is noxious to his refined respiratory system.

Not content to plunder discreetly the varied riches located in the Territories, Sloat, like Randall Flagg in The Stand, wishes to leave his indelible mark permanently on the landscape. Like some mad condominium developer unleashed without the restraint of zoning regulations, Sloat destroys the pastoral beauty of a whole section of the Territories--creating the Blasted Lands--an expansive valley of death that is the result of the nuclear radiation that Sloat and his Wolf henchmen send into the atmosphere in the form of giant fireballs:

>   Even in the moonlit dark he [Sawyer] could tell that the grain was thinning out, becoming

scrubby--about half an hour out of The Depot
the change had begun. Even the color seemed
wrong now, almost artificial, no longer the
beautiful organic yellow he had seen before,
but the yellow of something left too near a
powerful heat source--the yellow of something
with most of the life bleached out of it . . .
   Then he had noticed, even in the dark, how
the trees were stunted and bent; then he had
noticed the smell. Probably this had been
slowly growing in his consciousness, but it
was only after he had seen how the few trees
scattered on the black plain had coiled
themselves up like tortured beasts that he
finally noticed the faint but unmistakable
odor of corruption in the air. Corruption,
hellfire. Here the Territories stank, or
nearly.
   The odor of long-dead flowers overlaid
the land; and beneath it, as with Osmond, was
a coarser, more potent odor. If Morgan, in
either of his roles, had caused this, then he
had in some sense brought death to the
Territories, or so Jack thought. (462-463)

   Ironically, as Jack Sawyer rides his night
train further west, into the "future" of the
Territories, he passes life-forms that mark
distinct elements of de-evolution. As we have
already traced in The Mist and "Trucks," the
affiliation between technology and a prehistoric
past bears a dominant relationship in King's mind.
Thus, even as Jack moves toward Morgan Sloat's
nuclear future in the Territories, he finds
himself being pushed back into a reptilian
wasteland of the distant past that closely
resembles the transformed landscapes of The Mist
and "Trucks":

   The creatures falling behind the train
flattened out on the ground like snakes.
Their heads were doglike, Jack saw, but their
bodies had only vestigial hind legs and were,
as far as he could see, hairless and tailless.
They looked wet--the pink hairless skin
glistened like that of newborn mice. They
snarled, hating to be seen. It had been these
awful mutant dogs that Jack had seen on the

> banks of the railway cutting. Exposed, flattened out like reptiles, they hissed and snarled and began creeping away--they too feared the fireballs and the trails the fireballs left on the earth . . . . In the last of the flaring light from the ball of fire, the manlike being scuttled around the side of its dwelling. A thick reptilian tail swung from its hindquarters, and then the thing had slipped around the side of the building, and then it was dark again and nothing--dogs, man-beast, shed--was visible. (465-466)

The visual detailing of Morgan Sloat's nuclear handiwork represents the best writing in The Talisman. Throughout the novel, every event of any consequence that occurs in the United States is purported to produce some sort of parallel reaction within the mythical Territories. The Blasted Lands are the only occasion where the Territories may well be both a reflection of the nuclear tests conducted by the Army in Arizona and Nevada, as well as a dark prognosis for America's larger future. Perhaps this is the reason the Blasted Lands are depicted so vividly in The Talisman: King and Straub required little imagination to envision the results of radiation poisoning, a nuclear winter that King at least feels will be technological man's legacy to the earth:

> What had made such monstrosities? Nuclear damage, Jack supposed, since scarcely anything else had such power to deform nature. The creatures, themselves poisoned from birth, snuffled up the equally poisoned water and snarled at the little train as it passed.
> Our world could look like this someday, Jack thought. (471)

As Jack Sawyer journeys through Morgan Sloat's reconstruction of the Territories, he is disgusted and depressed by the transformation he observes. As Sloat argued early in the novel to Jack's father in justifying the introduction of sophisticated weaponry into the Territories, the defilement of the land is the price of progress--

the recreation of America in the pollution of the Territories.

Throughout his fiction, King measures imaginatively the price of such progress. The warnings he offers in his "tales of technology" bear much in common with Jack Sawyer's sobering worry that "Our world could look like this someday." For King, the distance between what he perceives fictionally and what modern America is doing to itself environmentally narrows on a daily basis, so that one of King's own great fears is that Sawyer's "someday" could be today.

In one of King's early, pseudonymous works as Richard Bachman, Roadwork, bulldozers, cranes, and other engines of destruction distinguish their forward progress through the reckless defoliation of the land. The people who are apparently operating the machines are sketched as mindless, pathetic drones doing only what they are instructed. George Dawes, the novel's protagonist, sabatoges the construction equipment in the hope that the roadwork will be aborted. In the conclusion of the novel, Dawes's efforts prove to be only temporary delays to the advancing design of progress. It is clear, in tales as diverse as The Talisman and "Trucks," that Stephen King has been rewriting Roadwork for the past two decades.

Chapter 3
The Fall from Grace:
Sexuality and the Corruption of Innocence

"Love is the enemy."
--George Le Bay

    Stephen King writes novels that are larger than life. He clearly owes both his considerable fame and fortune to scenes of graphic terror that are vividly rendered. But holding true to two of the most influential genres on King's own work--gothic romance and popular pulp fiction--King also relies rather heavily on frequent and explicit sexual references. Unlike much of the work in the gothic and pulp traditions, however, King seldom employs these scenes of sexual contact for the mere purpose of titillation; rather, he uses sexuality as a means to help highlight significant themes relevant to a specific story. He often likewise incorporates a character's sexual response as a way of signalling his or her place on the moral continuum of good and evil.
    Some of the sexuality found in King's books is portrayed in a positive fashion. King occasionally uses sex as a pure and ennobling act to contrast the surrounding evil and ugliness of a particular environment. In the novella <u>The Mist</u>, for example, David and Amanda make love in a supermarket while the building is under seige from a prehistoric reptile attack. Their lovemaking is in defiance of the violation which surrounds them; it is a re-assertion of human love and the need for physical contact in an environment that remains in stark opposition to these values.
    In <u>It</u> Beverly Marsh makes love to each member of the Losers' Club in an affort to secure the group's identity by bringing it together under this shared experience. She performs her unselfish act in order to forge an "<u>essential human link between the world and the infinite, the only place where the bloodstream touches eternity</u>" (1082-3). In failing to orgasm inside of Beverly (1083), however, Stan Uris does not complete "the circle," forfeiting the protective immunity from It that is afforded the other boys. His later suicide will indicate the full measure of his vulnerability. Thus, King's fictional use of sex

sometimes appears in the form of a salvation; it forms a preventative bond against evil.

Similarly, in *'Salem's Lot* the sexual encounter between Ben Mears and Susan Norton focuses our attention on a pure and innocent act of love, and is meant to serve as a contrast with the necrophilic blood lust of the vampires who have taken over the town. And in The Stand Nadine Cross knows that by making love to Larry Underwood she would be effectively insulated from Flagg's malevolent design. She understands, too, that the only way to break the dark man's evil bond is by surrender of her virginity to another man: "'Make love to me and that will be the end of it. I'll be safe. Safe. I'll be safe'" (496). On the other hand, when the former rock star, unaware of the importance behind her plea, chooses to spurn her advances, Nadine's descent into evil is fully determined: "'When all the choices but one have been taken away, what do you do?' You choose what's left. You choose what ever dark adventure was meant for you'" (500). Larry's decision to reject her pushes Nadine toward Flagg. As she walks away from Larry, her corruption is symbolically ordained in King's symbolic description of the landscape around her:

> She didn't turn around. She was a black shape distinguishable from other black shapes only when she crossed the street. Then she disappeared altogether against the black background of the mountains. He called her name once again and she didn't answer. There was something terrifying in the way she had left him, the way she had just melted into that black backdrop. (496)

Each of these examples presents sexuality in a role as a potential salvation from the isolation and sterility of evil. These examples notwithstanding, this perspective is the exception in King's fiction; he usually presents sex in a more negative light. It is most often a manipulative, enticing force that pushes characters toward greater levels of depravity. As the sexual relations become more frequent and more intense, the attraction to evil becomes correspondingly stronger.

In "Strawberry Spring" King links sexual arousal with the forces of nature. Medieval symbolism frequently invests the strawberry with sexual significance. Hieronymus Bosch's "Garden of Earthly Delights," for example, is resplendent in the fruit; indeed, sexual promiscuity has transformed certain individuals in his painting into walking strawberry hybrids. In an apparent inversion of Bosch's moral scheme, King's Strawberry Spring fog has transformed itself into a <u>femme</u> <u>fatale</u>, capable of inciting a dark passion that leads the narrator to commit acts of violence against college co-eds. The fog is an evocative presence, described as "dark and mist-blown. . .smelling of the sea, silent and deep" (173). Supported by other allusions found elsewhere in the text, this description is suggestive of a woman's hair and perfume. Like a mysterious lady, King's fog only comes out at night and can be seen ". . . moving silent and white along narrow college avenues and thoroughfares" (171-2). Indeed, the relationship between humanity and fog is personified in marital terms that go on to imply an unholy alliance between an amorphous, feminine evil and a sexually vulnerable male:

> Springheel Jack was a man, no one seemed to doubt that, but the fog was his accomplice and it was female . . . or so it seemed to me. It was as if our little school was caught between them, squeezed in some crazy lover's embrace, part of a marriage that had been consummated in blood. (177)

The narrator is obviously enchanted by this erotic, misty "lady," and is lured into acts of evil while under her spell. King's protagonist succumbs to the perverse sexual lure of this ambiguous feminine fog and commits a series of murders while under "her" influence. The narrator in this short story is a direct descendent of Keats' forlorn knight in "La Belle Dame Sans Merci." The lure of sex is used as a method of punishment and control: the knight and his modern relative, while not destroyed by their involvement with evil, relinquish their free will and become prisoners to a vaguely defined feminine force.

Like King's protagonist, who loses his sense of geographical and moral direction inside the fog's embrace, Keats' knight is a man trapped in a dreary landscape, lost in "The latest dream I ever dream'd/ On the cold hill's side" (ll. 35-6). In the surprise conclusion of the tale, where the narrator reveals himself to the reader as Springheel Jack, the sexual emphasis maintained throughout the story is given an added dimension as the narrator's wife accuses him of having an affair, "'She thinks I was with another woman last night. And oh dear God, I think so too'" (180). The other woman he speaks of is not only an ironic reference to the females he has killed, but also enlarges to include the sexual association he has formed with the feminine presence embodied in the Strawberry Spring.

King's early novel <u>Carrie</u> is a study in the unresolved tensions that accompany the transition from adolescence to adulthood. The novel's abundant use of blood symbolism--from Carrie's first menstrual period to the pig's blood that crowns her at the prom to the blood that Carrie herself and the town mutually shed during her night of carnage--parallels the book's focus on Carrie's own emerging sexuality. It is, after all, Carrie White's failure to understand her own sexuality that puts in motion the events which will eventually destroy both Carrie as well as the town that has tormented her. Carrie's innocence produces a confused response to her body's menstruation, and this sexual innocence is meant to contrast with the sophistication of the other women who torment her, especially the supremely evil Chris Hargenson.

Unlike Carrie, Chris is fully aware of what sex means, the potential power it represents, and of her ability to use it to her own advantage. She employs her body to manipulate the males in her life. She started with older, college men while she was in high school:

> They began by treating her with patronizing good fellowship . . . and ended up trotting after her with panting, doglike lust. If they trotted long enough and spent enough in the process, she usually let them go to bed with her. (128-9)

In light of Chris's attitude toward sex, her relationship with Billy Norton emerges as something sleazy and negative. When they initiate sex in his car, Chris tells Billy: "'Feel me all over. Get me dirty'" (132). Although Billy is already a criminal, it is Chris who seduces him into further evil: ". . . it was she who suggested that William Nolan and his friends make the trip to Irwin Henty's farm" (109). Like the narrator in "Strawberry Spring," who is submerged in a passion that is out of his control, Billy is victimized by Chris's sexual domination. His participation in the abuse of Carrie White is motivated by the power of lust:

> It was for Chris Hargenson, just as everything was for Chris, and had been since the day she swept down from her lofty college-course Olympus and made herself vulnerable to him. He would have done murder for her, and more. (112)

As sex with Chris becomes more frequent and more intense, Billy loses whatever control he once possessed over his own actions. At the end of the novel, he is little more than a mirror to Chris herself--mimicking her worst impulses, helping to carry out her darkest and most violent fantasies. Indeed, their final scene together describes their sexual behavior in terms that suggest a barroom brawl. Just as they have preyed upon Carrie's weaknesses with animal-like cruelty, the bestal imagery used to describe their descent into a sexual union shortly after humiliating Carrie shows the full measure of their depravity:

> It was 11:20 P.M. when Christine Hargensen and Billy Nolan got back to The Cavalier. They went up the back stairs, down the hall, and before she could do more than turn on the lights, he was yanking at her blouse.
> . . . He slapped her, rocking her head back. Her eyes took on a flat and deadly shine.
> "This is the end, Billy." She backed away from him, breasts swelling into her bra, flat stomach pumping, legs long and tapering in her jeans; but she backed toward the bed. "It's

over."

"Sure," he said. He lunged for her and she punched him, a surprisingly hard punch that landed on his cheek.

He straightened and twitched his head a little. "You gave me a shiner, you bitch."

"I'll give you more."

"You're goddam right you will."

They stared at each other, panting, glaring. Then he began to unbutton his shirt, a little grin beginning on his face.

"We got it on, Charlie. We really got it on." He called her Charlie whenever he was pleased with her. It seemed to be, she thought with a cold blink of humor, a generic term for good cunt." (212-3)

As each of these illustrations demonstrates, King's purpose in describing the sexual lives of many of his characters is to supply the reader with a visual manifestation of corruption. Since a healthy sexual response should be an affirmation of life and love between human beings, the perversion of that bond serves as an effective vehicle for portraying the loss of one's humanity, a surrendering to sin. In King's fiction when sex is used as a vehicle for manipulation, its consequences are always evil; when sexuality serves a demented will, the passion of love is turned into the aggression of self-destruction.

In *The Stand*, Randall Flagg's influence over Nadine Cross is predominately sexual in nature. As her resistance to his will weakens, she, like Billy in *Carrie*, becomes more evil (signified by her hair turning white and her willingness to deny the voice of her conscience in order to plant the bomb which will destroy the members of the Free Zone committee). When King's characters are seduced by the corruption of perverse sexuality, they lose their identity and the ability to control their own destinies. After Flagg completes the violation he has ordained for Nadine by physically raping her in the desert, her soullessness is an extreme representation of what happens to every King character who is warped by sexual manipulation:

> She was pregnant. If she was also catatonic, what did that matter? She was the perfect incubator. She would breed his son, bear him, and then she could die with her purpose served. After all, it was what she was there for. (676)

The association between evil and sexuality in _The Stand_ is a web that extends from Flagg to include Harold Lauder as well as Nadine Cross. Flagg uses Nadine's corporeality to complete Harold's spiritual corruption. Significantly, the origins of his fall can be traced to a point early in the book as Harold watches Fran and Stu engage in sexual intercourse:

> Neither of them saw Harold, as shadowy and as silent as the dark man himself, standing in the bushes and looking at them. Neither of them knew that his eyes squinted down into small, deadly triangles as Fran cried out her pleasure at the end of it, as her good orgasm burst through her. (359)

Harold interprets Frannie's willingness to make love to another man as an act of personal betrayal. Like Milton's Satan, equally enraptured and frustrated by Eve's beauty, Harold's personality for the remainder of the book is shaped by his intense jealousy, and King certainly implies that Harold's resolve to strike out against the Free Zone was born at the very moment Frannie and Stu made love.

If Lauder's moral poisoning begins with his reaction to Frannie's sexual "betrayal," his decadent interludes with Nadine solidify and refine his affiliation with evil. Not only does Nadine prey upon Harold's viginity, tempting him with promises of sensations he has never before experienced, she likewise encourages his penchant for sexual perversion:

> "We can do things. Things you've never even... no, I take that back. Maybe you _have_ dreamed of them, but you never dreamed you'd do them. We can play. We can make ourselves drunk with it. We can wallow in it. We can..." She trailed off, and then did look at

him, a look so sly and sensual that he felt himself stirring again. "We can do anything--everything--but that one little thing. And that one thing really isn't so important, is it?"

Images whirled giddily in his mind. Silk scarves. . . boots . . . leather . . . rubber. (520-1)

It is significant that Nadine's "one little thing" is forever denied to Harold. The fact that Lauder technically dies a virgin, never having actually participated in intercourse, serves to highlight his failure to view sex as anything more than a self-enclosed act--its sole purpose, his own physical release. As Nadine is willing to accommodate him only with her mouth, she is nothing more than an extension of Harold's cronic urge to masturbate. As such, she serves Flagg's evil perfectly, as the dark man thrives on human isolation and the pursuit of selfish desires. (The reader may recall that Flagg's two central henchmen--Trashcan Man and Lloyd Henreid--are supreme examples of alienation, and that Flagg gains the loyalty and service of each through promises of conquest and greater arenas of destruction.)

In the first of many oral sexual encounters, Harold's orgasm is linked to death: "It took less than a minute. He cried aloud with the strength of his climax, unable to help himself. He could understand why so many writers made that connection between orgasm and death" (520). After he and Nadine have severed forever their connection to the Free Zone, Harold is no longer of any use to Flagg's design--in fact, he threatens it. Thus, after his "accident" on the highway while heading west, Harold's decision to commit suicide merely concludes the death pact he initiated months earlier in accepting Nadine as his lover. Indeed, his method of committing suicide is even reminiscent of Nadine's acts of fellatio: "He put the muzzle of the Colt into his mouth and looked up at the blue sky" (666). His sexual lusts have left Harold openly vulnerable, and in the end he is betrayed by his failure to discipline them:

He had seen himself as the king of anarchy, but the dark man had seen through him and had reduced him effortlessly to a shivering bag of bones dying badly by the highway. He lay there with buzzards swooping and diving on the thermals overhead, trying to rationalize the unspeakable. He had fallen victim to his own protracted adolescence, it was as simple as that. He had been poisoned by his own lethal visions. (666)

Generations of grade-B horror films have argued with a single, dogmatic intensity that human sexuality is a precarious pursuit; indeed, that the curious young men and women who stray naively into this murky area of experience do so at the risk of terrible consequences. As King has argued in <u>Danse Macabre</u>, the horror genre is a notoriously conservative one where non-conformity and experimentation of any kind are thoroughly exorcised:

> I've tried to suggest throughout this book that the horror story, beneath its fangs and fright wig, is really as conservative as an Illinois Republican in a three-piece pinstriped suit; that its main purpose is to reaffirm the virtues of the norm by showing us what awful things happen to people who venture into taboo lands. Within the framework of most horror tales we find a moral code so strong it would make a Puritan smile . . . . The horror story most generally not only stands foursquare for the Ten Commandments, it blows them up to tabloid size. (368)

The horror genre is especially puritanical in its repression of sexuality. Nearly every act of brutality that occurs in the deathless installments of the <u>Friday the 13th</u> saga, for example, directly follows some sort of pre-marital sexual encounter between a scantily clad teenage cheerleader and her clean-cut captain-of-the-football-team boyfriend. Thus, amidst the severe anti-social behavior that represents the superficial thesis of most horror films, the audience also receives a moralistic sub-text: sex of any sort, especially the pre-marital variety, is punishable by death and/or something worse. "Sex," continues King in <u>Danse Macabre</u>,

> makes young adolescent boys feel many things, but one of them, quite frankly, is scared. The horror film in general, and the Vampire film in particular confirms the feeling. Yes, it says; sex <u>is</u> scary; sex <u>is</u> dangerous. And I can prove it to you right here and now. Siddown, kid. Grab your popcorn. I want to tell you a story . . . . (77)

As we have seen in illustrations throughout this chapter, King probes the affiliation between sex and sin to its furthest extreme. Unless human sexuality is motivated by unselfish love, it always serves the larger design of evil. In <u>The Shining</u> and <u>Christine</u>, sex is both a conduit in which evil disguises its sinister intentions under a cloak of seduction and the only visible manifestation of the abstract principle itself. I will have more complementary observations to make regarding King's perception of women elsewhere in this book, but it is interesting that Christine and the ghost woman who dances with Jack Torrance in <u>The Shining</u> are, like the fog in "Strawberry Spring," versions of a depraved feminine sexuality. These particular feminine associations are indicting examples of King's own contributions to the fundamental conservatism of the horror genre.

It is unfortunate that the majority of King's negative illustrations of sexuality highlight the woman's role as modern Eve: an amoral seductress devoted to perverting men. It is unfortunate because this is a narrow view of womanhood and it simply reinforces the madonna/whore stereotype that has helped to sustain the general distance which continues to exist between men and women. In a later chapter of this book we will consider the madonnas of King's fiction and how they serve as moral counterbalances to the whores. The fact still remains, however, that there are few complex women in his canon--women who are multi-dimensional blends of good and evil. King's focus in dramatizing the human struggle between good and evil is centered exclusively on men or boys, as there are no women characters who undergo the same ambitious level of intellectual and moral embattlement that we see within Larry Underwood, Louis Creed, Jack Torrance, or even Jack Sawyer. His women are, finally, reminiscent of many female characters found in nineteenth-century literature: hobbled to the stereotype of being either divinely good or diabolically evil--but never a blending of the two.

Early in the novel *Christine*, Dennis Guilder is suspicious about the secret attraction a 1958 Plymouth Fury holds for his friend Arnie Cunningham. When Dennis seeks information about the car and former owner's histories, Le Bay's brother tells him that "'love is the enemy . . . . Love is the old slaughterer. Love is not blind. Love is a cannible with extremely acute vision. Love is insectile; it is always hungry'" (91). We have seen this definition of "love" in operation in many of King's portraits of human sexual relationships. In *Christine* Arnie Cunningham falls in love with a car, but this inanimate object comes to exert a level of control over Arnie that is identical in its oppressiveness and its defilement to the human sexual relationships discussed elsewhere in this chapter. Moreover, Christine's gradual dominance over Arnie is continually expressed in sexual imagery. Dennis comments on how quickly Arnie is ravished: ". . . he had been like a man who meets a showgirl, indulges in a whirlwind courtship, and ends up with a hangover and a new wife on Monday morning. It had been . . . well . . . like love at first sight" (63).

Throughout the novel Arnie is torn between his love for Christine and his love for Leigh and Dennis. There is even a jealous rivalry between the "girls," as Leigh accuses Arnie of loving the car more than her. And there is certainly cause for Leigh's comparison. Arnie responds to Christine on a highly charged sexual level; when he touches the car, "the touch turned into a caress . . . . He ran his hand slowly over the dashboard, loving the feel of it" (253). Even Dennis senses a sexual undercurrent to the car, and his dream exposes the image of sexually excited female, undulating her hips: "[the] car lunged forward a little each time the engine revved, dropped back, lunging forward again, the hood vibrating" (65). But perhaps the best example of the sexual affinity between Arnie and his feminine machine occurs on the day in which he is forced to push Christine back to Darnell's garage after the car's vandalization:

> . . . he had pushed her until the sweat ran off him in rivers and his heart thudded like a runaway horse in his chest and his back cried out for mercy; he had pushed her, his body pumping as if in some hellish consumation; he had pushed her, and inside the odometer ran backward, and some fifty feet beyond the door his back began to really throb, and he kept pushing, muscling it along on the flat, slashed tires, his hands going numb, his back screaming, screaming. And then--
> He reached Christine and flung himself inside, shuddering and panting . . .feeling the calm slowly wash through him like a soothing balm. He touched the steering wheel, let his hands slip down it, tracing its delicious curve. (320-1)

Clearly King means to imply, even symbolically, that Arnie attains an orgasm in the act of pushing his car. The breathless prose, "his body pumping," the sweat pouring off him, all building to a climax--inside the car's leather upholstry--where everything is suddenly calm. The interior of Christine is paralleled with a woman's vagina: soft, warm, comforting.

But Christine, like the fog in "Strawberry Spring," uses a disarming sexuality to entrap her men. This novel is built upon the fundamental masculine distrust of femininity. Christine is a male version of the American female as she is frequently portrayed in films and magazines: The Vamp--sexually alluring but nonetheless treacherous. <u>Christine</u> echoes the love/hate relationship that men have always had with women: "Oh he loved her and loathed her, he hated her and cherished her, he needed her and needed to run from her, she was his and he was hers . . . " (319). The story of Arnie Cunningham's stupration merely gives credibility to the majority of male-oriented rock lyrics that introduce each chapter:

a reminder of what happens when a man surrenders himself completely to feminine sexuality. Arnie loses his only hope for salvation when he relinquishes his bond with Dennis in order to join in a marriage that aligns him with Le Bay, Satan, and the feminine engine from Hell.

The evil of the Overlook Hotel, like the regenerative mechanism of Christine, has no definitive origins or loci. In several early chapters of The Shining, expunged from the first edition by Doubleday in an effort to streamline the novel but later published under the title Before the Play, King provides some insight into the history of the hotel's ownership. This history is severely clouded by violence and gruesome accidents. But there is yet another common thread that links together each of the three owners King discusses: each man became so obsessed with the Overlook that he was willing to sacrifice the health of his finances as well as that of his marriage to remain in contact with the hotel. The personification of the Overlook, like Christine, is associated with a definite feminine sexual presence. The Overlook is a mistress for each of these owners, challanging not only the sanctity of their marriages, but their sanity as well:

> Bob T. had fallen in love with the hotel as an idea, and his love had deepened as the hotel took shape, no longer a mental thing but an actual edifice with strong, clean lines and infinite possibility. His wife had grown to hate it--at one point in 1908 she told him that she would have preferred competing with another woman, that at least she would have known how to cope with-- . . . . (20-1)

Like the three owners of the Overlook who sell their souls for her love, Jack Torrance is mentally and physically seduced by the evil of the hotel. There are several ways of interpreting Jack's breakdown during that long winter in Colorado, but surely his self-destructive collapse is due in part to the hotel's ability to subvert the marriage bond he shares with Wendy. Long before their arrival at the Overlook, Danny senses that divorce is a very real possibility for his parents: "Daddy's DIVORCE thoughts were more complex, colored dark violet and shot through with frightening veins of pure black. He seemed to think they would be better off if he left. That things would stop hurting" (28). The Overlook merely exploits this marital weakness. In fact, it is at the point where Jack's gradual mental seduction by the hotel becomes physical--when the hotel assumes the shape of the beautiful ghost-woman--that the thoroughness of Jack's corruption is manifested:

> She was tall and auburn-haired, dressed in clinging white satin, and she was dancing close to him, her breasts pressed softly and sweetly against his chest. Her white hand was entwined in his. She was wearing a small and sparkly cat's-eye mask and her hair had been brushed over to one side in a soft and gleaming fall that seemed to pool in the valley between their touching shoulders. Her dress was full-skirted but he could feel her thighs against his legs from time to time and had become more and more sure that she was smooth-and-powdered naked under her dress,
> (the better to feel your erection with, my dear)
> and he was sporting a regular railspike. If it offended her she concealed it well; she snuggled even closer to him. (346)

King seems to be indicating here that in the dissipation of his marital commitment to Wendy, Torrance forsakes his only chance for survival. It is, after all, the loyalty of love--connecting Danny and Wendy, the shining, Danny and Hallorann--that allows them to escape the hotel's apocalyptic fate. Prior to the above quoted scene, when the Overlook's seduction is restricted to a purely psychological assault, Jack shows a certain capacity for introspection--he is aware of, even participates in, his own disintegration-- and is thus in a position where he might conceivably exert some measure of control against the will of the Overlook. But when the hotel assumes the actual shape of a lascivious woman in order to complete Jack's corruption, his willingness literally to dance with death (as well as to become sexually aroused by it) signals his capitualtion to self-destruction. His violation, in other words, is once again consummated in sexual terms; he has betrayed his marriage, his child, and his career in order to become one with the spectral mistress. He is owned by the forces of the Overlook--body and soul.

Like Harold Lauder, the narrator in "Strawberry Spring," and Arnie Cunningham, the evil residing in the Overlook employs sexuality to pervert Jack's moral conscience and to sever his connection to humanity. In their respective failures to resist sexual entrapment, each of these men is subsumed by evil, becoming an extension of its corruption. They are finally modern Adams, who, instead of only losing the Garden of Eden, have also relinquished their self-respect, the love of Eve, and the hope of any reconciliation with God.

Chapter 4
The Shape Evil Takes:
Hawthorne's Woods Revisited

>"Is not this better," murmured he, "than what we dreamed of in the forest?"
>"I know not! I know not!" she hurriedly replied.
>--*The Scarlet Letter*, 236

Stephen King's fictional allegories owe much of their formulation to, and are reminiscent of, the romance tradition in nineteenth and twentieth-century American literature. There are at least two occasions in *Danse Macabre* where King acknowledges his debt to Hawthorne's tales. In his discussion on the origins of *'Salem's Lot*, for example, King tells us that he "wanted to try to use the book partially as a form of literary homage . . . working in the tradition of such 'classical' ghost story writers as Henry James, M.R. James, and Nathaniel Hawthorne" (37-8).

Like Poe, Melville, Hawthorne, and Flannery O'Connor, King often places his protagonists in situations where they encounter the reality of evil, and from this encounter they must make choices which will influence the remainder of their lives. How his characters react to the loss of innocence is a central theme in King's work; their ability to survive is dependent upon what they learn from the fall from grace.

As is so often the case in Hawthorne's canon, the awareness of sin forces King's characters to proceed in one of two possible directions. The first is toward moral regeneration, a spirit of renewed commitment to other human beings that is born from an acceptance of the devil's thesis as postulated in "Young Goodman Brown," that "Evil is the nature of mankind" (98), and that the failure to acknowledge either the existence of evil or its nexus to mankind results in spiritual death. On the other hand, the discovery of sin can frequently be overwhelming; it does not always lead to a higher state of moral consciousness. In Hawthorne and King, the encounter with evil is often portrayed as an experience that leads to isolation and self-destruction. Characters in their fictions commit their worst transgressions in refusing to recognize the evil in themselves, and in failing to exert a greater measure of self-discipline.

Dr. Louis Creed, the protagonist in Stephen King's 1983 novel <u>Pet</u> <u>Sematary</u>, shares much in common with the darkest characters in Hawthorne. Creed is similar to the impassioned, but misguided idealists who populate Hawthorne's stories; he resembles Aylmer, Rappaccini, Chillingworth, Goodman Brown and Hollingsworth who also fail to recognize the inviolable distinction separating human idealism from the limitations of reality. Like these characters in Hawthorne, Creed violates standards for personal moral conduct and brings about his own destruction.

Early in the novel we learn of Doctor Creed's perspective on death. In response to his daughter's anger over the prospect of someday losing her cat to the mysterious force that has populated the Pet Sematary, Creed responds that "'Clocks run down--that's all I know. There are no guarantees, babe'" (36). Creed's controlled attitude toward death infuriates both his daughter and wife. They see nothing "natural" in the abrupt negation of life. But more important, the novel will also reveal that Creed himself does not believe that death "'is the most natural thing in the w[orld]'" (41). His disciplined attitude is merely a veneer that is shattered when his own child is killed. When confronted with the reality of his child's death, Creed displays his inherent inability to maintain a rational perspective towards immortality. After Louis loses his only son, he seeks to repudiate death's dominion over the human world by availing himself of the resuscitative energies residing within an Indian burial ground located in the woods several miles behind his home.

In the nineteenth century, Emerson and the transcendentalists assured their audience that nature represented a vehicle to true self-knowledge. King and Hawthorne certainly concur with this premise, although the self disclosed by Thoreau in the pines at Walden pond is vastly different than what Louis Creed and Goodman Brown uncover in the wilderness behind their respective communities. Instead of a mirror to the self's purity and limitless potentiality that the transcendentalists associated with New England nature, the woods of Hawthorne and King are a reflection of the self's essential darkness and the human affinity to sin.

The journey into the wilderness in Hawthorne's fiction is always fraught with danger. Within the New England pines of Hawthorne's symbolic landscapes we find the powerful rhythms of primordial and uncontrollable forces. Hawthorne's Puritan ancestors fully comprehended that within the uncut trees surrounding their early enclaves lurked elements that were seldom benevolently disposed toward human welfare. In the woods, one could easily lose direction, encounter hostile Indians and animals, or worse yet, be forced into an immediate struggle with Satan's legions. As Heinrich Zimmer explains in The King and the Corpse,

> The forest has always been a place of initiation for there the demonic presences, the ancestral spirits, and the forces of nature reveal themselves. The forest is the antithesis of house and heart, village and field boundary, where the household gods hold sway and where human laws and customs prevail. It holds the dark forbidden things--secrets, terrors, which threaten the protected life of the ordered world of common day. (69)

The Scarlet Letter, "Roger Malvin's Burial," "Young Goodman Brown" and "Ethan Brand" all mirror the Puritan influence on Hawthorne's work. When the protagonist in each of these tales ventures forth into the forest, he returns to his respective village and family in a transformed state. Within the New World forest, Hawthorne imagined a bifurcated vision: the danger of Faustian temptation as well as the possibility for rebirth and transcendence.

Dimmesdale and Reuben Bourne are made to face the realities of their own self-deceptions in the woods; the journey into the dark pines becomes a metaphor for a journey into the self. Separated from the hypocritical pressures of civilized life, Dimmesdale and Bourne acknowledge the true depravity of their natures; from this profound recognition of the evil within themselves, each man emerges from the woods chastened, his life dramatically altered.

Like Dimmesdale, Reuben Bourne is living a lie; his failure to provide Roger Malvin with a Christian burial, coupled with his unwillingness to tell Dorcas the truth about her father's abandonment in the woods, create "a moody and misanthropic man . . . feeling few regrets and disdaining to acknowledge any" (19). In order to confront his sins and gain forgiveness for them, Bourne must re-enter the woods and acknowledge his repressed guilt: " . . . in the calmest and clearest moods of his mind, he was conscious that he had a deep vow unredeemed, and that an unburied corpse was calling to him out of the wilderness" (17). The wilderness serves Bourne in a psychoanalytic capacity; by forcing him into contact with that part of himself that he has willfully denied, Reuben's journey takes him deeper into the woods--and by symbolic extension, deeper into himself: "[he] strayed onward rather like a sleepwalker than a hunter" (22). Hawthorne's use of a somnambulistic analogy is important here, as it highlights the function of the woods as a representational arena for the unconscious self, the place where Bourne confronts his darkest impulses, and where civilized hypocrisies are finally stripped clean. As Reginald Cook argues in "The Forest of Goodman Brown's Night: A Reading of Hawthorne's 'Young Goodman Brown,'" Hawthorne's symbolic forests reveal the very turbulence of the human mind, "the form its guilt takes, the contributions of grace and election, the sense of justice, the invocation of mercy" (478).

Over the years, Bourne's sins have corroded his soul: "[his] insulated emotions had gradually made a selfish man, and he could no longer love deeply except where he saw or imagined some reflection or likeness of his own mind" (19). Since Bourne recognizes in his young son Cyrus, "what he himself had been in other days" (19), his child's murder serves as a symbolic death of Bourne himself--the destruction of that part of his psyche, long sustained by a posture of deceptive innocence, which has produced his guilt and anxiety. Bourne's purification is achieved at the expense of his son's life in order to appease "a voice audible only to himself, commanding him to go forth and redeem his vow" (18). In satisfying this primitive "voice" that Reuben hears deep in the woods, his son's blood opens the way to the civilized virtues of exculpation, reconciliation, and a renewal of his Christian faith.

Young Goodman Brown and Ethan Brand are also profoundly changed by their experience in the woods, but for these characters the struggle against the evil they discover there is not positively resolved. Neither Brown nor Brand is spiritually transformed by the insights they gain in the forest; in fact, unlike Dimmesdale or Bourne, Brown and Brand forfeit the opportunity for personal salvation when they reject their bond with the community of sin openly acknowledged in the woods.

Louis Creed's journey into the trees behind his house shares more in common with the negative voyages in "Young Goodman Brown" and "Ethan Brand" than with the redemptive encounters portrayed in "Roger Malvin's Burial" and The Scarlet Letter. King's Wendigo, the wrathful Indian spirit that animates the unholy Micmac burial ground beyond the Pet Sematary and footfall, exploits human weakness and vulnerability; it thrives on the doctor's inability to discipline his curiosity and to recognize the distinction between saving lives and playing god. As is the situation in Hawthorne's tales, the woods in King's novel reveal man's penchant for evil, his innate depravity; but unlike the forests of "Young Goodman Brown" or The Scarlet Letter, which offer at least the possibility for spiritual advancement concurrent with an acceptance of personal sin, the wild god of King's wilderness makes no such compromises with Louis Creed. Hawthorne's natural landscapes appear to be animated by subtle forces that ultimately invite his protagonists into a confrontation with ethical codes and principles. As "Roger Malvin's Burial" illustrates, the trek into the woods often serves as an unsentimental journey toward moral instruction. In contrast, King's Wendigo is thoroughly amoral: it manipulates human trust through the promised miricle of resurrection--only to deliver a grotesque version of itself.

Goodman Brown and Ethan Brand discover that the forest is much darker and more ominous than they originally anticipated, and Louis Creed eventually gains a similar insight. Each time the doctor ventures into the Indian cemetery, he, like Brown and Brand, experiences a greater level of human estrangement. The encounter with evil narrows each of these men into a position where they become less sensitive to the "magnetic chain of humanity" (285) and more involved with themselves and their own personal quests. Brown's wandering into the woods reveals a progressively deepening awareness of the pervasiveness of evil. The revelation that his perspective on the nature of his community, clegy, ancestors, and even his wife has been naive and inaccurate, pushes Brown from a state of innocence to one of cynical despair. Unable to accept the reality of evil in either humankind or himself, Brown "shrank from the bosom of Faith; and at morning or eventide, when the family knelt down at prayer, he scowled and muttered to himself, and gazed sternly at his wife, and turned away" (100).

As Brown's encounter with evil produces a retreat into himself, Louis Creed's deepening involvement with the dark powers of the Wendigo likewise alienates the doctor from his own family and community. Indeed, Creed's obsession with bringing his son back to life is indulged at the expense of his other, nearly catatonic child and desolate wife: "There had been times in the dark watches of the night when she [his wife] had longed to hate Louis for the grief he had fathered inside her, and for not giving her the comfort she needed . . . " (324). Contemplating a second trip to the burial ground to bring about his son's resurrection, Louis Creed's isolation finds a parallel in Goodman Brown's "dying hour [of] gloom" (100) and Ethan Brand's break from "the universal throb . . . of brother man" (285):

> That feeling of coldness still held; he felt totally unplugged from his people, the places that had become so familiar to him, even his work. . . . Madness was all around him, softly fluttering as the wings of night-hunting owls with great golden eyes: he was heading into madness. (278)

In the fictions of Hawthorne and King there are definite realms of experience that highlight man's limitations, his inability to grasp, much less to manipulate, the mysteries found in nature and deep within the human heart. Hawthorne's idealists engage actions that violate moral barriers--whether in the form of perverse scientific quests (as in "The Birthmark" and "Rappaccini's Daughter") or through personal intrusions into the secrets of another human being (as in the actions of Chillingworth and Ethan Brand). Terence Martin observes in "The Method of Hawthorne's Tales," that "the cancer of obsession threatens any Hawthorne character--scientist, man of religion, artist--who prefers an idea to a human being" (17). Louis Creed's self-corruption occurs as a result of a similar transgression: he consciously chooses to liberate the malevolent energies residing in the Micmac burial ground because he wishes control over nature's greatest secrets--the ability to regulate life and sustain existence.

Like Hawthorne's doctors, Aylmer and Rappaccini, Creed sacrifices the people who are dearest to him because of his obsession with an idea: the challenge of altering the immutable laws of nature. While it is possible to argue persuasively that Creed is initially drawn to the Micmac burial site because of an altruistic love for his daughter and the desire to spare her the pain of grief over a lost cat, by the conclusion of the novel altruism is no longer the doctor's primary motivation. Creed's compulsion to deliver the bodies of his son and wife to the cemetery is not adequately explained as a consequence of his guilt and grief. Rather, he is more interested in continuing his misguided experiment under the irrational premise that eventually he will discover a way to dominate death. At various points throughout the book Creed appears to be keeping an unconscious personal record against death. Each time his medical skills aid in saving a human life, Creed whispers to himself, "'won one today, Louis'" (161). Creed's game against the reaper continues even as the stakes grow ever larger. Although he has listened to repeated warnings about the treacherous nature of the place and has even witnessed first hand the monstrous consequences of his son's resurrection, the doctor remains convinced of his ability to manipulate the powers residing in the burial ground. As a result of his refusal to accept the workings of Fate, he is transformed into an extension of the amoral Wendigo. Like the insistent Aylmer in Hawthorne's tale "The Birthmark," who willingly squanders his beautiful wife for the sake of testing a scientific theory, Creed sacrifices himself and those around him in his obsession to unlock the mystery that will yield the secret of immortality: "'I waited too long with Gage,' Louis said. 'Something got into him because I waited too long. But it will be different with Rachel, Steve. I know it will'" (370).

In spite of the mechanistic world-view maintained in most gothic fiction, the characters in King and Hawthorne still possess a persuasive element of free will. The majority of their protagonists are like Louis Creed: they choose their own course of action. It is an act of Ethan Brand's own volition that leads him to pursue the Unpardonable Sin, just as Goodman Brown's gloom is a result of his choice to emphasize only the "despair" and none of the "triumph" voiced by Satan's congregation in their communal awareness of evil (98). As Robert Deamer points out in "Hawthorne's Dream in the Forest," "[Brown] did not <u>have</u> to journey into the forest and to indulge in doubts of Faith or in visions of orgiastic evil. Faced with the choice of loving his wife or believing in his religion, he chose, disastrously for him, to do the latter" (334).

While it may be true that the Micmac burial ground possesses, as Jud Crandall asserts, "'a power . . . and it's coming around to full again'" (246), Creed freely elects to avail himself of its insidious magic. He essentially acknowledges his terrible freedom moments before he begins his son's disinterment: "his heart told him quietly and absolutely that he couldn't come back tomorrow. If he didn't do it tonight, he could never do it. He would never be able to screw himself up to this crazy pitch again. . . . This was the moment, the only time for it he was ever going to have" (297). Moreover, Creed makes his decision to re-enter the enchanted woods in a flagrant rejection of Victor Pascow's prophetic warning. Pascow's recent death provides immediate insight into the malevolence which resides in the Indian burial ground, and he tries in vain to share this vision with Creed: "'The door must not be opened. . . . The barrier was not meant to be broken. Remember this: there is more power here than you know. It is old and always restless. . . . Your destruction and the destruction of all you love is very near, Doctor'" (70).

In light of Creed's election to disregard Pascow's message, it is interesting that Jud Crandall, who is responsible for introducing the doctor to the transformational properties inherent in the Micmac soil, is soon placed in a position to employ its life-giving powers. After learning that Norma, Jud's beloved wife, has died suddenly, Creed's first thought is of "Jud pulling Norma's corpse on a pagan litter through the woods. Toward the Micmac burial ground beyond the Pet Sematary" (173). But unlike Creed, Jud is capable of exercising a greater measure of self-control; he rejects the temptation to resurrect Norma. His memory of Timmy Baterman remains a vivid illustration of the Wendigo's devastating influence over human interments, and this recollection serves as a sufficient deterrent to keep Jud from further experimentation. Not only is Crandall capable of restraining the selfish impulse to play God by summoning Norma back to life, but he also supplies Creed, after the latter loses his son, with advice that echoes Pascow's warning: "'You know why I'm here,' Jud said. 'You're thinking about things that are not to be thought of, Louis. Worse still, I fear you're considering them'" (230).

Throughout Hawthorne's fiction, his protagonists are offered sage counsel and guidance during the course of their moral struggles. In "My Kinsman, Major Molineux" a friendly stranger encourages Robin to seek alternatives to the patronage of his kinsman or a return ticket home. Mary Goffe reminds Richard Digby of his relationship to other human beings and tries to lure him away from his isolation in "The Man of Adamant." Similarly, Hester Prynne is Dimmesdale's model of endurance and courage in The Scarlet Letter. And in "The Birthmark" Aminadab, Aylmer's laboratory assistant, immediately identifies the danger inherent in his employer's quest to remove Georgiana's facial flaw, muttering to himself, "'If she were my wife, I'd never part with that birthmark'" (209). Each of these characters parallels Jud Crandall's role in *Pet Sematary*: they are presented as sensible counterpoints to the encroaching madness of the central protagonists. Like Jud, they embody the human requisite to recognize and exercise a measure of control over the self's most debased and indulgent urges. Moreover, they offer unsentimental alternatives to the main character's choice of action, reminding him of obligations that challenge the limitations of egotism. If their examples and/or advice is emulated, the protagonist usually endures; if rebuffed, self-destruction is the inevitable consequence.

In *Pet Sematary* Stephen King captures the native speech patterns, the elements of life in a cold climate, and the specificity of place that set his readers firmly in a rural Maine world. King is a regionalist for many of the same reasons that Hawthorne chose to write about Massachusetts: each author understands that the universal themes of great literature--human sin, fear, and endurance--can only be rendered truthfully within settings and by personalities an artist has come to know on a first-hand basis. Much as Hawthorne relied on Puritan New England as a setting to describe the foibles and sins that are the inheritance of humanity, King views Maine as a deliberate backdrop for his own allegories, enabling him to utilize specific elements from that culture in his portrayal of the moral conflicts common to us all.

The events which transpire in the woods behind the Pet Sematary are reminiscent of the narrative pattern which occurs in Hawthorne's fiction. An individual loses his innocence in the encounter with tragic circumstances and is faced with the struggle to redefine himself morally. In portraying the negative results of this struggle, both writers suggest that there are certain mysteries man must simply learn to accept, certain secrets he has no business attempting to discover, and certain ethical barriers that he only transcends at the expense of his soul. Hawthorne's tales and King's novel achieve their power in demonstrating that one's humanity is dreadfully easy to lose, and what we abandon ourselves to possess, we necessarily become. The romantic poet William Blake may have felt perfect harmony residing in "the lineaments of gratified desire," but for King and Hawthorne the inevitable end of such self-absorption is the madness of Louis Creed circling back through the woods for another trip to the Micmac burial grounds or the devastation of Ethan Brand's marbled heart.

Chapter 5
The Divine and the Damned:
Tom Cullen and Trashcan Man

"We fall from womb to tomb, from one blackness and toward another, remembering little of the one and knowing nothing of the other . . . except through faith."
--<u>Danse Macabre</u>, 380

The cosmic conflict between the forces of good and evil has been a staple theme of mythology and literature since Beowulf and Grendel first clashed in a poet's imagination. One might argue that this struggle is at the very heart of literary history; perhaps the monsters and their slayers have changed names and forms down through the centuries, but the essential allegorical shape of this conflict has remained intact. And we, the simultaneously delighted and apprehensive listeners of these dark tales, remain fascinated with the implications behind each one of these clashes. The horror and fantasy writer, by virtue of his acute awareness of an allegorical romance tradition, is in an excellent position to place this metaphysical struggle in a modern context.

Stephen King is one of the great writers of magical realism. He posseses the unique ability to structure tales of fragile and ordinary human beings embattled against supernatural forces they neither comprehend nor can hope to surmount physically. Their dramatic plights, however, always unfold in the most believable environments available--a supermarket, a 1958 Plymouth Fury, an expansive Colorado hotel, the backwoods of a Maine suburb. As we have traced in Chapter 1, King understands the importance of maintaining a fictional world with which the reader can both identify and embrace as his own. After establishing such a relationship, King's portrayal of the conflict between good and evil-- which is finally the issue at the core of every one of his major tales--attains a level of acute believability.

King's themes can be found in the hackneyed and derivative material of paperbacks written by a host of less talented writers that flood the aisles of local supermarkets--yet another demonic possession, yet another Victorian mansion that refuses to give up the ghost. The King imitators--John Skipp and Craig Spector's <u>The Cleanup</u> is a lamentable case in point--are composing grade-B movie scripts, not writing literature. Dishonest in the presentation of plot, one dimensional in character portrayals, supermarket horror is too often long on special effects and short on literary value and substance. And this is where King differs most markedly from other writers in the field.

The post-apocalyptic setting of a deserted American landscape in <u>The</u> <u>Stand</u> provides a fitting arena as good and evil again battle for control. This particular confrontation has been viewed by various readers as a struggle between God and the devil, between Mother Abagail and Randall Flagg, between the politically liberal community of Boulder, Colorado and the repressive regime of Las Vegas, Nevada. But on its most interesting level, this novel is also a study in the struggle between the differing ethical alternatives available to human beings. There are two individuals in this book who epitomize the respective moralities of the two societies from which they emerge--Tom Cullen from the Free Zone and Trashcan Man from Las Vegas. Tom represents the spirit of hope that is finally the greatest legacy of the Free Zone, while Trashcan Man embodies the urge toward destruction that is emblematic of Flagg and his Las Vegas denizens.

Tom Cullen's basic goodness represents the hope for humanity on which the whole notion of the Free Zone resides, both as a temporary sanctuary for the lost citizens of a destroyed world and as the antithesis to Flagg's colony in Las Vegas. Tom Cullen is mentally retarded, leaving him naive, intellectually a child forever. This connects him to other children in King's fiction, the Danny Torrences, Jack Sawyers, and the various members of the Losers' Club, whose innocence and uncorrupted states enable them to overcome the destructive forces they encounter.

Since Tom is not afflicted with the post-plague consciousness that is present among the other survivors, he is still able to savor the simple joys which remain in the world. In this sense, his limited perception may be a blessing. A simple toy brightens his whole day, and when Nick gives him a bike, Tom Cullen becomes the happiest person still living in the decimated remains of the United States. As Nick observes, the two weeks during which Tom makes the journey westward may have been the most contented of his entire life, for in the company of Andros, who has also been an outsider and victim of society's cruel taunts, Tom finds acceptance and love:

> For Tom, Nick reflected, these last two weeks had probably been the happiest of his life. He was with people who accepted and wanted him. Why shouldn't they? He might be feeble, but he was still a comparative rarity in this new world, a living human being. (342)

The disability that had alienated Tom from others is no longer such a factor. Yet this innocent, naive state allows him to transcend the misery of the moment. He possesses an intuitive appreciation for the loyalty, the courage, and the friendship necessary for survival in this world where all values, formerly taken for granted in organized society, are now subject to question.

When Cullen is placed under hypnosis in preparation for his assignment as a spy in Flagg's camp, he reveals intimations about the dark man and Mother Abigail that astound the others. Clearly, Cullen is in the tradition of the sainted idiot, whose purity of soul provides him with a direct conduit to God. Indeed, at one point Tom acknowledges that he is no longer the same boy who began the journey westward with Nick Andros, instead he reveals that he is now "'God's Tom'" (532). Indeed, the boy-man possesses a perfect harmony with all of God's creation: "During the afternoon, a large rattlesnake crawled in beside [Tom] to get out of the heat of the day. It coiled itself by Tom, slept awhile, and then passed on" (698). Tom is guided in his journey out of the desert by Nick's spiritual presence toward a mystical hand (the Hand of God? Stu wonders bemused) that appears on the horizon--two of the most convincing moments in this book that lend support to Mother Abigail's conception of a benevolent diety.

Once in Las Vegas, Tom remains immune to Flagg's powers of omniscience. Not only does Flagg's extrasensory perception fail in detecting Tom, but Flagg cannot instill the fear in Tom that he is able to exert in others. Because of this, Tom is able to assess the situation in his own innocent and accurate way. His conclusion about the people who are part of Flagg's Vegas empire is the most perceptive and terse analysis offered by anyone in the Free Zone:

> When he got back to the Zone--if he did get back to the Zone--he would . . . bask in the love of his friends. That was what was missing in Las Vegas, he decided; simple love. They were nice enough people and all, but there wasn't much love in them. Because they were too busy being afraid. (702)

This contrasting emphasis on love and fear are the key differences between Tom Cullen and the society of Boulder and Trashcan Man and the people in Las Vegas. Tom Cullen appears to be slow, mentally retarded, and generally inferior to "normal" people. Yet inside Tom is a strong love for Nick, Stu, Glen, and the other individuals he knows in Colorado. It is this love that gives him the strength to overcome the obstacles in his way. His innocence, the only effective counterbalance to Las Vegas' corruption, insulates Cullen from Flagg's powers of intimidation. With the aid of his extra perception, speaking to him in the desert through the voice of Nick Andros, Tom is able to locate and rescue Stu Redman from certain death by carrying him to safety and then nursing him back to health.

The qualities of unselfish love and commitment to others are essential elements of the Free Zone state and represent the primary reasons for its survival. The Free Zone may be unorganized, it is slow in re-establishing Boulder's electrical services, the democratic political system re-surfaces with all its cumbersome checks and balances, and the state does not have a marshal until Stu Redman is elected against his desires, but the Free Zone nonetheless endures because its citizens share a common goal and a common commitment. They are willing to give of themselves, to sacrifice themselves if necessary, for the greater good of the community. Whether it is the volunteers blistering and lacerating their hands at the power plant, the workers on the burial crew engaged in the hard and unpleasant task of burying the dead, or Judge Harris, Dayna Jurgens, Larry Underwood, Glen Bateman, and Ralph Brentner who willingly sacrifice themselves, the Free Zone survives because people give of themselves for what they believe. Each of the individuals mentioned above <u>chooses</u> the fate and/or labor that is necessary for the life of the whole society; no one has to force them into making these difficult decisions. It is in this capacity for unselfish love that King sees the hope for humanity's future. This is a core premise that operates not only throughout <u>The Stand</u>, but also in the writer's eloquent recommendation in <u>Danse Macabre</u> for belief in an alternative to existential despair:

> I believe that we are all ultimately alone and that any deep and lasting human contact is nothing more nor less than a necessary illusion--but at least the feelings which we think of as "positive" and "constructive" are a reaching-out, an effort to make contact and establish some sort of communication. Feelings of love and kindness, the ability to care and empathize, are all we know of the light. They are efforts to link and integrate; they are the emotions which bring us closer together, if not in fact then at least in a comforting illusion that makes the burden of mortality a little easier to bear. (25-6)

In Las Vegas, as Glen Bateman reminds his fellows citizens, Flagg "'has got the trains running on time and all his ducks in a row'" (396). The electricity is on, the weapons are in place, the pilots are training, and the city is cleansed of burdensome drunks like Rick Moffat. But beneath this surface veneer of social and technological discipline is a turbulent and self-destructive reality. Mother Abigail senses this undercurrent though she has never been to Las Vegas and makes her observations from many miles away: "She guessed that behind the conscious evil there was an unconscious blackness. That was what distinguished the earth's children of darkness; they couldn't make things but only break them" (403).

Donald Merwin Elbert, also known as Trashcan Man, epitomizes the state of the Las Vegas society. On the surface, Trash appears to be under Flagg's complete control. He is an amoral, technological genius who is thrilled at the prospect of working for Flagg and will gladly carry out the dark man's every command. Yet if we examine the reality beneath both the man and his city, we see profound problems.

In Las Vegas everything operates out of fear--fear of the Walkin Dude, Randall Flagg. Even his right-hand man, Lloyd Henreid, is terrified of him. Moreover, the citizens of the city are so fearful that they can sense when he is present and when he has left. Flagg may be able to leave the drugstores unlocked, but that is only possible because the penalty for an addiction is crucifixion. People refrain from drinking anything stronger than beer because they are afraid they will say something that will be self-indicting. This is a society based on total subjugation of the will of the people. And since Vegas operates under the tyrannical oppression of its leader, the people take their cue from Flagg himself. Thus, unlike the Free Zone, there is no spirit of trust in Las Vegas--anyone is susceptible to death for the smallest infraction.

> Far away over the mountains was another cloned creature. A cutting from the dark malignancy, a single wild cell taken from the dying corpus of the old body politic, a lone representative of the carcinoma that had been eating the old society alive. One single cell, but it had already begun to reproduce itself and spawn other wild cells. For society it would be the old struggle, the effort of healthy tissue to reject the malignant incursion. But for each individual cell there was the old, old question, the one that went back to the Garden--that of free will. Over there, in the west, all the old hates and fears were spawning themselves. The

assassins of Eden were there, the dark fusilliers. (427)

Flagg's volatile temper keeps Lloyd Henreid and the other bureaucrats at the MGM Grand from supplying their leader with advice or information which may run counter to his intentions. This lack of communication eventually proves fatal to Flagg's design, as it did once a generation earlier for Adolf Hitler's, for even with his omniscent powers, the dark man cannot be everywhere at once; his unwillingness to delegate real authority to others and to deal rationally with set-backs to his plans finally dooms his dream of conquest. Indeed, Flagg's flag never gets beyond the Las Vegas city line.

An entire society and individual men and women may be able to exist under such conditions for a period of time, but when the balance of control is inevitably shaken, chaos will ensue. This is precisely what occurs to Trashcan Man. Within his character we find not only the seeds, but the very method of destruction, for both Las Vegas and himself.

Trash's history is one of pain and misery. His father killed his brothers and sister and then Trash witnessed his father's murder at the hands of the man who would later marry his mother. During all this time he was severely ridiculed by his peers, not only for these events over which he had no control, but also for the pyromania which was a psychological response to his abuse:

> The voices all became phantom voices, but the rocks were impossible to ignore when they came whizzing from the mouths of dark allies or from the other side of the street. Once someone had pegged a half-full can of beer at him from a passing car and the beer can had struck him on the forehead and had driven him to his knees. (184)

Life is a vicious circle of violence and humiliation leading Trash to commit greater acts of incineration and anarchy. Trashcan Man's negative reception from the world is motivation enough for his anti-social disposition, employing his society's greatest and most prized resource--

technology—against itself. Like one of Faulkner's warped characters—Joe Christmas or Popeye—Trash's identity was molded into its perverted form by a perverse society and by a Fate clearly at odds with human needs. When Trashcan Man is atop the petroleum tank preparing his timed explosive device, he views a bug lying in a puddle of gasoline, and he thinks to himself,

> I'm like that bug, he thought resentfully, and what kind of a world was it where God would leave you stuck in a big sticky mess like a bug in a puddle of gas? It was a world that deserved to burn, that was what. He stood, head bowed, a third match ready to strike when the breeze died . . . .
> From behind a perfect fusillade of explosions, God's ammunition dump going up in flames of righteousness, Satan storming heaven, his artillery captain a fiercely grinning fool with red, flayed cheeks, Trashcan Man by name, never to be Donald Merwin Elbert again. (183, 188)

If Nick Andros, Tom Cullen, Stu Redman, Larry Underwood, and the other members of the Free Zone rediscover their essential connection to humanity in their respective journeys westward, Trashcan Man's humanity is all but tortured out of him in his own dark journey into isolation. The fractured wrist, the badly burned arm, the painful falls from the bike, the desert heat, the dehydration, the constant morphine high, and the grisly voyage through the corpse-ridden Eisenhower Tunnel, all but insure Randall Flagg that Trash will arrive in Las Vegas completely insane.

Although Trashcan Man and Tom Cullen would appear to be diametrically opposed characters, existing at the extremes of a moral scale, they actually share a set of interesting similarities. Both Tom and Trash are essentially innocent victims of society and nature. As a result of Tom's retardation (an accident of fate) and Elbert's various humiliations at the hands of a callous humanity, both men are estranged from the larger community and its societal interrelationships. Moreover, they maintain similar levels of comprehension regarding the way in which the world operates; neither character is capable of functioning very well on his own. As a result of these mutual correspondences, Trash and Cullen are extraordinarily receptive to the attention Flagg and Nick Andros bestow on them. It is plausible to assume that Flagg and Andros are the first individuals to express any genuine interest in either man. Thus, the loyalty their attention inspires remains unchallenged and unqualified: "'My life for you'" (716), Trash repeats over and over in his prophetic oath to Flagg, while Tom dreams about Nick for weeks after the latter's death.

But it is also important to note that Nick and Flagg respond to aspects in Tom and Trash that correspond precisely to their own personalities. Tom represents the limitless depth of kindness that Nick evinces in his ability to forgive the street punks who assault him early in the novel. Although Andros is perhaps the most intelligent member of the Free Zone founders, he, along with Mother Abigail (who immediately senses his uniqueness), is the Boulder society's best illustration of love as a guiding principle to life. Also, like Tom, Nick is handicapped--deaf and dumb--and thus is immediately sympathetic to Tom's own afflictions. Consequently, Tom and Nick complement one another--Nick possesses the intellect Tom has been denied, while Tom is the physical presence that Nick will work through to save Stu Redman's life.

Just as Cullen is an extension and reflection of Andros' fundamental personality, Trashcan Man represents the most self-destructive impulses found at the heart of Flagg's character: "Lloyd had seen Flagg lay his hands on Trashcan Man's shoulders and tell him gently that all the dreams had been true dreams" (681). The dark man is drawn to Trash for two reasons: first, he longs to employ Trash's technological expertise. Like Trash, Flagg seeks to reactivate the sophisticated weaponry of the pre-plague world in order to see the remains of civilization engulfed in flames. Secondly, in providing Trashcan Man with absolute freedom to roam the American waste land, Flagg is essentially giving vent to the destructive impulses of his own id. Trash is emblematic of the core anarchy that is just beneath the tyrannical exterior of Flagg's character. The latter can no more regulate Trashcan Man's impulsive actions than he can regulate his own temper or penetrate Tom Cullen's innocent insulation.

Since the last third of the novel shows evidence of Flagg out of control, it is appropriate that Trashcan Man should bring about the annihilation of the Las Vegas empire. As Freud often cautioned in his analyses of the self-destructive potential centered within an undisciplined id, Trashcan Man incinerates himself, his surrogate god, and their mutual dream of technological conquest. Indeed, Flagg's hope that Trash's technological expertise will help him in the destruction of the Free Zone go spiralling down with the shattered and charred remains of both the helicopters and pilots that Trash blasts out of the sky:

> And Trashcan Man. He had thought he could dismiss Trash entirely. He had thought Trashcan Man could be thrown away like a defective tool. But he had succeeded in doing what the entire Free Zone could not have done. He had thrown dirt into the foolproof machinery of the dark man's conquest. (699)

It is therefore fitting that Trashcan Man should bring about the final, catastrophic conclusion to Flagg's dark design. In his final scene in the novel, Trashcan Man's physical state is an ultimate metaphor of Flagg's own spiritual condition and that of his society as well. Trash arrives in Las Vegas towing an atom bomb, vomiting up his teeth. His already ravaged body is covered with open sores: "He looked like a man who had driven his electric cart out of the dark and burning subterranean mouth of Hell itself" (762). Trash's advanced case of radiation sickness is symptomatic of both the ironic failure of Flagg's technological hopes and the social cancer that exists in the Vegas society--the latter, a place where relationships are modelled on a master-servant prototype, where fear is the only social glue holding the society together, and where the hope for atonement is centered around materialistic gifts of incredible destruction.

In the end it is Tom Cullen's unflagging love for his friends and his quasi-mystical connection to God which allow him to survive his journey to and from Las Vegas when no one else could. His faith and his kindness underscore the very qualities of the Free zone which insulate it from the ravages of evil. Moreover, like the idiot savant in Russian icons, Cullen's vision of truth is eventually realized by the other menbers of the Free Zone whose powers are comparatively limited.

Trashcan Man and Randall Flagg. Tom Cullen and Nick Andros. These are the polar opposites on King's moral continuum. His other characters appear to fall somewhere in between these representatives of absolute selfishness on one hand, and divine love on the other. In the course of a particular tale, King's characters are severely tested by both human and supernatural temptations. Those, like Arnie Cunningham, Harold Lauder, Greg Stillson, and Richard Sloat, who sacrifice their moral freedom for the ultimate attraction of accumulating power at the expense of love, descend into themselves and die ignominiously. Their demise is unmourned by the rest of the world, because these men have lived only for themselves, becoming human manifestations of the evil principle King sees in constant battle against whatever moral forces also animate the universe. King's moral citizens--the inhabitants of the Free Zone, Jack Sawyer, Danny Torrance, the members of the Losers' Club, and a growing chorus of male writers and maternal women--are uniquely opposed to the model of violence and corruption represented by Randall Flagg. Tracing the alternatives available for moral survival in King's fiction constitutes the second half of this book.

Part Two:
And Those Who Are Left to Tell the Tale

>The drama's done. Why then here does any one step forth? --Because one did survive the wreck.
>--Epilogue, Melville's <u>Moby-Dick</u>

To this point, <u>The Moral Voyages of Stephen King</u> has focused primarily upon analyzing incidents of moral breakdown and spiritual bankruptcy in the fiction of Stephen King. As the previous chapter on Tom Cullen and Trashcan Man illustrates, there exist moral absolutes in the writer's perception of how the world is arranged. Spiritual degeneration occurs when these absolutes are violated in some manner. Just as Louis Creed, Jack Torrance, Randall Flagg, and Trashcan Man are examples of individuals who have aligned themselves with evil, and as a consequence are destined for self-destruction, other individuals in King's fiction somehow manage to insulate themselves from evil's corrosiveness. The remaining chapters of this book explore the dynamics of survival in King's canon. His heroes and heroines appear to share at least one thing in common: In contrast to evil's ability to isolate and reduce the individual to selfish pursuits (e.g. Creed's obsessive interest in the regenerative powers of the Pet Sematary, Harold Lauder's quest to relieve his own insecurities through the subjugation of others), those who resist such temptation do so by establishing a highly disciplined code of priorities that places friends, children, and, in the case of King's author-protagonists, the act of writing in a position superior to the self and egocentric desires. Like so many writers of Christian allegories before him--from Milton and Dante, to Shakespeare and Hawthorne--King's fiction is a warning about the dangers inherent in the sacrifice of others for the gratification of private impulses. If evil in King's universe can be defined as a principle of negation directed at everything that exists outside the self (ironically poisoning the very self at its center), then goodness must necessarily be its opposite--the force of selfless commitment to others. In Part One of this book we have observed examples of moral dissolution, psychological perversity, and horrific phenomena that are often brought into existence because the individual relinquishes the capacity to control his baser instincts and thus submits to errors in human judgment. Part Two of <u>The Moral Voyages of Stephen King</u> examines the survivors in the writer's canon: those men and women who establish meaningful lives for themselves and those they love in the face of malevolent forces and circumstances which initially appear greater than their human capacities for endurance.

Chapter 6
Speculations from the Locker Room:
Male-Bonding and Non-Traditional Families

"I've never been able to comprehend why any adult American male would rather be with his best buddy rather than his girlfriend on a Saturday night."
--Kathy Ann McCarthy, 1974

The creation of memorable characters is one of the strongest elements in Stephen King's literature. Unlike so many financially successful examples of current popular fiction--the cosmetic worlds of Judith Krantz, the sexually decadent, emotionally vapid interludes of Sidney Sheldon, or the equally repulsive nouveau riche men and women who prowl the expensive boutiques and boulevards of Jackie Collins--King's characters are just like the rest of us. They are basically middle class men and women struggling to get along. As King himself has acknowledged while attempting to define his own popularity to Douglas Winter in an interview published in Faces of Fear:

> In most cases, [my] characters seem very open and accessible. They seem like people that you would like to know, or even people you do know. People respond to that, and there is very little of that in novels today. . . . In most of the books, I think, there's a kind of Steve King hammock that you fall into--and you feel really confortable in that hammock, because you know these people and you feel good about them. You don't have unease about who they are; you have unease about the circumstances that they find themselves in. And that's where the suspense comes from. (251)

Since King's characters exist in the same world as his readers, they are beset by familiar problems: divorce, alcoholism, loneliness, financial anxieties. The majority of King's adolescents come from single-parent families, or, like Danny Torrance in The Shining, have experienced first-hand the trauma of marital discord. As with so many of King's young people, the gradual dissolution of the Torrance marriage forces Danny to act older and more responsibly than his years would appear to allow. The central plots of tales as diverse as "The Boogeyman," Cujo, The Shining, Thinner, and Pet Sematary revolve around the breakup of the American nuclear family. One of the primary attractions of King's adolescent protagonists is that they are so often essentially alone; their parents are off fighting with one another or wallowing in self-pity, while the children grow up in a vacuum punctuated only by random moments of affection. Our sympathies are naturally drawn to a Gordie Lachance or Jack Sawyer or Carrie White because we sense their vulnerability . . . as well as their immediate relevance to the unstable status of modern marriages in America. The products of broken homes and distracted parents, King's children attempt to fill the emotional void created by the fractured family. Searching for an emotional stability which the nuclear family can no longer offer, the male characters in King's work form bonds with one another to create their own nontraditional families. There are no comparable relationships for King's women; same sex bonding in his fiction remains an exclusively male domain. Carrie White and Charlie McGee, for example, are left decidedly on their own. As the next chapter will examine, his female characters obtain access to similar nurturing bonds only when they enter into the realm of motherhood.

In The Shining the special power of the shine is communicated between two male characters, Danny Torrance and Dick Hallorann. Their shine provides them with the ability to communicate telepathically and to foretell the future. Since they share this unique talent, they are immediately drawn to each other.

Danny's power to shine often belies his loneliness and isolation. Believing that he is the only individual to possess this gift (or curse), Danny's attitude toward it is a mixed one: He is both attracted to the special insights Tony provides, and mistrustful of them; indeed, while Tony often shows him things he desires to know, he likewise places words in front of the child that he cannot read. Moreover, he knows his parents have deep misgivings about Tony. Hallorann, however, is proud of this unique talent--and he shares his perspective with Danny. The Overlook's history of sin and depravity will lure Jack into a blood communion that will cost him his life. Hallorann also possesses a psychic history of his own, but unlike the sinister traditions in place at the Overlook, the black man's supernatural correspondence was with his grandmother. It is a memory that warms the chef even as he shares its recollection with Danny: "'You got a knack,' Hallorann said, turning to him. 'Me, I've always called it shining. That's what my grandmother called it, too. She had it. We used to sit in the kitchen when I was a boy no older than you and have long talks without even openin our mouths'" (81).

The discovery of Hallorann and their shared abilities encourages the bond of a special friendship. As Danny wanders through the abandoned halls of the Overlook, "He kept discovering little flashes of Dick Hallorann's personality lying around, and they reassured him like a warm touch" (168). The relationship between Hallorann and Danny not only saves the boy and his mother from certain destruction at the hands of Jack and the other specters who reside at the hotel, but serves as an effective counterbalance to the force of negation embodied within the Overlook. The communication afforded through the shining allows Danny to summon Hallorann from one end of the country to the other. "'You'll make it,' Hallorann said. 'We'll all make it'. . . Hallorann burst through the double doors and carried the two of them through the trench" (432).

The male bond that develops between Danny and Hallorann, however, merely begins with their escape from the Overlook. Once Danny has left the nightmare of the Overlook's ghosts and his father's degeneration back in Colorado, the real healing must begin. Hallorann is there as a symbol of strength and a promise for the future:

Hallorann said, "You'll grieve for your daddy, but see to it that you get on. That's your job in this hard world, to keep your love alive and see that you get on no matter what.

Pull your act together and just go on. . . ."
He put an arm around Danny's shoulder and the
boy reeled the fish in, little by little.
Wendy sat down on Danny's other side and the
three of them sat on the end of the dock in
the afternoon sun. (447)

This final scene in the novel is certainly
one of hope: Hallorann's encouraging advice
appears reflected in his physical presence next to
Danny. The family unit is restored, Wendy on one
side, Hallorann on the other, Danny in the middle.
King makes us feel that the chef will assume the
role vacated by Jack: that of Danny's moral
guardian and mentor. Indeed, this nontraditonal
family unit, consisting of a black man, white
woman, and white boy, will serve as the nucleus
for a new beginning for Wendy and her son,
allowing them to put the nightmare of the Overlook
behind them.

Unlike the Hallorann-Torrance bond, Gordie
and Chris in King's novella The Body are not
united through psychic powers. Their association
emerges to fill a mutual void created by the
absence of parental support and their fierce
desire to escape Castle Rock's society. While
their families play cruel, or at best, indifferent
roles in their lives, Gordie and Chris become each
other's surrogate parent and confidant.

Chris's desire to leave Castle Rock centers
around his morally corrupt family. The Chambers
have worked hard to maintain a reputation of
failure: "Chris came from a bad family, alright
and everybody thought he would turn out bad . . .
including Chris. His brothers lived up to the
town's expectations admirably" (303). Unwilling
to provide their son with any measure of
encouragement or support, Chris's parents merely
want him to uphold the traditional Chambers model
of drunkenness and defeat. In contrast to his
natural family, Gordie makes Chris realize that he
has the potential to leave Castle Rock and escape
the pattern of failure epitomized within his
family. The young man helps Chris to recreate a
new family in their mutual rejection of the
existing institutions within Castle Rock's
community:

> We both dated through high school, but no girl ever came between us. Does that sound like we went faggot? It would have to most of our old friends, Vern and Teddy included. But it was only survival. We were clinging to each other in deep water. I've explained about Chris, I think; my reasons for clinging to him were less definable. His desire to get away from Castle Rock and out of the mill's shadow seemed to me to be my best part, and I could not just leave him to sink or swim on his own. If he had drowned, that part of me would have drowned with him, I think. (449-450)

While not abused physically by his parents, Gordie, the "invisible boy," comes from a family which virtually ignores his existence because of their omnipresent grief over another son's loss. Even more insidious, his parents seem to hold their remaining son responsible for Denny's death. Chris, however, does not permit Gordie to internalize these feelings; instead, he urges him to use his talents as a writer and to avoid the natural tendency toward self-pity:

> "I wish to fuck I was your father!" he said angrily. "You wouldn't go around talking about takin those stupid shop courses if I was! It's like God gave you something, all those stories you can make up and He said: This is what we got for you kid. Try not to loose it. But kids loose everything unless somebody looks out for them and if your folks are too fucked up to do it then maybe I ought to." (393)

Each boy thus assumes the duties and responsibilities which normally fall upon the shoulders of the parents. Their mutual support system extends beyond mere friendship or loyalty--it is a bridge that transverses the chasm created by the absence of parental love and involvement.

In *The Talisman*, Jack, like Danny, Gordie, and Chris, develops male bonds which serve as the basis for an emotional support system. However, Jack's development includes the profoundly anti-social addition of an animal-human relationship. As Jack searches for the talisman, his survival is centered on another black man, Speedy, and a wolf.

Jack initially discovers the first of these male figures, Speedy, at a point of deep personal crisis. Like Danny in The Shining, Jack finds in the black adult the paternal consolation and guidance that has been missing since his father's demise. Alienated in his New Hampshire environment, Jack constantly fears for his mother's health. Death surrounds Lily and dominates her character. Jack is terrified by the thought that he will lose his mother after so soon experiencing the losses of his uncle and father, thereby leaving the boy totally isolated. Speedy's encouragement provides the child with the inner strength to cope with his anxieties: "Speedy Parker had become closer to him than any other friend . . . . And now, counteracting his terror at losing Uncle Tommy and fear that his mother was actually dying, he felt the tug of Speedy's warm presence" (10). Like Danny's relationship with Hallorann, Jack finds more than a friend in Speedy. Encountering him when the child can no longer hope to discover solace in his natural family, Speedy represents the nucleus of a new familial order.

Jack and Speedy, a white boy and a black adult. The combination appears out of place in the American landscape, and consequently they share a bond that is built on mutual fear and a kindred spirit of alienation. Their closeness does not evolve over time, but is fueled with the desperation of their respective situations: Speedy and Jack both know that the queens are in danger of dying.

A lost child, Jack thrives on Speedy's wisdom while Speedy requires Jack's hidden strengths in order to employ the talisman to save the Territories. Speedy wins Jack's trust and gives him the initiative to seek the talisman. However, Jack is still a frightened and immature child when he first encounters Speedy. Although the black man makes him acknowledge the need for the quest, Jack can comprehend the journey only in terms of his own life; he has yet to secure the understanding that the talisman represents the hope for salvation for two societies as well.

His bond with Wolf helps to enlarge Sawyer's scope to the point where he comes to understand his mission in terms of a responsibility to countless individuals. Where Speedy is Jack's teacher and source of inspiration, the relationship that forms between Jack and Wolf inverts Jack's role from passive child to an active boy-man in control of his own destiny. And Jack's sense of friendship and loyalty deepens from Wolf's dependency upon him. Wolf, in short, completes the moral education that Speedy begins: "There it was. Wolf was his responsibility . . . he had taken Wolf by the hand and dragged him out of the Territories and into Ohio. He had no choice" (297). Like the version of Jack himself we find emerging from the Oakley tunnel early in the novel--clinging to his toothbrush, yearning for his mother's comfort--Wolf is a foreigner in a strange land, and he must be directed and encouraged. Jack must learn to care for others beside himself, and just as he is responsible to Wolf because he brought the creature into a new world, Jack likewise learns that he owns a responsibility to whole countries because of his predetermined association with the talisman. As Michael Collings argues in *The Many Facets of Stephen King*,

> There may be pain in Jack Sawyer's world, and loss and death; but there is also restoration. Just as Frodo [from Tolkein's *Lord of the Rings*] emerges from his quest changed, or Ransom from his in Lewis's space novels, Jack Sawyer is changed. He has the power to heal and uses it wisely . . . . In doing so, he comes to understand his own reality more completely and confirms the need for right choice in both worlds; he learns simply to do a good thing. (134-135)

The relationship between Jack and Wolf shares many analogies in American fiction: the primitive and the civilized joined in a masculine blood bond that flaunts itself in the face of drawing room and institutions of social conformity. Melville's dark-skinned savages in his sea fiction, Natty Bumppo's link to Chingachgook the Indian scout, and of course, Huck and Jim on the Mississippi--

the blending of the primitive and the civilized is a dominant motif in mainstream American fiction. But for a moment, let's consider another parallel comparison from American literature to deepen the union Jack shares with Wolf.

In John Steinbeck's novel, <u>Of</u> <u>Mice</u> <u>and</u> <u>Men</u>, we find a similar correlation to Jack and Wolf. There is ample evidence that King has read and appreciated Steinbeck's fiction. Collings cites on two occasions King's admiration for Steinbeck's style and craftsmanship. Indeed, the several similarities in the writings of Steinbeck and King represent an entire vein of critical thought yet to be mined by the emerging writers of King scholarship.

King learned a good deal about the specifics of storytelling from his study of Steinbeck. There is a sense of gritty American realism in the respective styles of both writers. Neither tells a story of the charmed life of millionaires or movie stars. What the reader receives are struggles from ordinary people--those individuals who have built and lived by the American Dream only to find that, in some cases, the dream is nothing but an illusion. Their respective dialogues are rich in regional dialect and feeling. Their characters speak as real people do, encompassing a recognizable tone, diction, and colloquial figures of speech. And of course each author can be considered a painter of the American landscape; although forty years separate their work, the pictures each man created retain similar characteristics.

In <u>The</u> <u>Talisman</u> and <u>Of</u> <u>Mice</u> <u>and</u> <u>Men</u> Jack and George are put into analogous positions: they must exercise their authority and judgment or Wolf and Lennie will be destroyed by the world. This position is not always favored, and just as George remarks frequently that it would be so much easier without Lennie, so Jack contemplates a simpler journey without the nuisance of Wolf. While Wolf is not retarded like Lennie, he is in fact a wolf from the Territories, thus giving him the same simple-minded comprehension of the world that Lennie possesses. He also shares the characteristic of great strength with Lennie, as well as an unyielding adoration for his respective travelling companion.

What becomes one of the most important aspects of these two relationships is the attitude of unselfishness each partner demonstrates towards his companion. While George and Jack are the intellects who are placed in the position of guide, Lennie and Wolf use their enormous strength to protect. It is not a bullying technique and they are not fully conscious of the imposing threat their strength imposes. Nonetheless, at the slightest indication of any harm to their friends, these two "simple minds" would freely sacrifice themselves, and Wolf eventually does.

Another facet that cannot be overlooked is the love that Lennie and Wolf so freely give to George and Jack. Society seldom comprehends such a relationship based upon absolute trust and understanding, and a major cause for tension in both books is the failure of society to appreciate or approve the true beauty of these unions. Lennie and Wolf help George and Jack keep their faith in human nature; their innocence is like a protective shield against the lies and cynicism of the world.

Since there is no overt sexual connotation in either relationship, it is very important to highlight what love and emotions really mean in this context. American men characteristically are taught to suppress their emotions. It is the female who is permitted to cry at sad movies, while the strong man holds his passions under tight rein. Full expression of deep male emotion occurs only in the locker room or in the pages of American fiction. When the occasions arise, when men are able to share their deep feelings and be fully understood in meaning, a special bond is established. Steinbeck, King and Straub appear to appreciate that these unions are not easily arrived at, and so are not easily forsaken.

The relationships discussed in this chapter share common elements: an understanding between individuals that delves deeper than language, race, or citizenship; a commitment to one another that is often at the expense of a character's life; and, finally, a love bond that exists outside the perimeters of acceptable behavior in a heterosexual culture. These relationships are often illict, first of all because they consist of two males, and secondly, because of the inherent prejudice that society harbors against retardation, losers, and even wild wolves (a boy and his dog, maybe--a boy an his wolf, never). If there exists a certainty in American social life, it is the danger inherent in breaking or veering from the norm. Thus, these relationships remain in constant conflict with the larger society around them. While it is true that the breaking of the physical bond--Chris and Wolf are killed-- may occur in the course of the struggle, something else endures in the boy-man who survives. The memory of the male bond maintains itself and continues in its role as moral guardian and inspiration for life. This is why Wolf is magically able to "rejoin" Jack in the concluding pages of The Talisman: the beast may be physically dead, but his union with young Sawyer is perpetuated.

The types of nontraditional male relationships sketched in this chapter exist throughout King's canon--from the closeness Mark Petrie shares with Ben Mears in 'Salem's Lot to the extended family of adolescents who compose the Losers' Club in It. King keeps returning to these unions as a way to suggest an alternative to the corruption and treachery he views as the dominant features of the traditional American nuclear family. Like the male bonding discussed in this chapter, the next two chapters will focus on relationships of survival. The myriad of maternal-child bonds, the many examples of protagonists-writers' life-sustaining commitments to their work, and the male-to-male friendships already discussed suggest deeply autobiographical elements from King's own life.

Having grown up without a father, King may well be developing through his fiction strategies for coping with the absence of a traditional patrimony. It is interesting to note, in light of this discussion, that most images of the patriachy in King's fiction--from religious and social institutions to actual father figures such as Jack Torrance and Billings in "The Boogeyman"--are portrayed in a negative light. In The Shining, surely King's best illustration of the destructive capabilities of the father, Jack Torrance's fury against his family merely reflects the Overlook's general attitude toward its inhabitants. Although the hotel often disguises itself in feminine sexual imagery (see Chapter 3), its guiding impetus is still predominately masculine--a managerial hierarchy that manifests its will through acts of physical violence.

In "Before the Play," King's elaborate history of the Overlook expurgated from the novel itself by King's editors at Doubleday, the hotel's first owner, Bob T. Watson, loses his son in a suspicious horse riding accident. Although his wife urges him to abandon his obsession with the hotel in order to comfort her in her grief, he refuses: "'You've put that hotel up in the tabernacle of your heart!' She assured him in a shrill voice. 'Built it on the bones of your first-born son!'" (22). Watson joins the other Overlook fathers, Delbert Grady and Jack Torrance, as evidence of a patriarchy that is both callous and out of control. The Shining is about the separating of weak males from the balancing influence of their more sensitive womenfolk and children. Thus, King's characters--particularly his children--are left, like Danny Torrance, to seek solace and the bonds of paternal affection through avenues other than the traditional nuclear family.

The experience of parenthood seems to produce opposite reactions in King's men and women. While the men often appear constrained in their roles as fathers, the following chapter will reveal how his women achieve a new personal significance through the fulfillment that attends pregnancy and motherhood. King's own mother, Nellie, at least as she is described in the "Notes Toward a Biography" chapter of Winter's The Art of Darkness, exercised a tremendously positive influence during the formative years of the writer's life. Against the strain of financial difficulties and without the assistance of a husband, Nellie King managed to hold her family together with love. The short tale "The Woman in the Room" is about her son's feelings at her death in 1974.

King's perception of motherhood also owes something to raising three children with Tabitha, his wife, who remained with him through the days when they could not afford to pay the telephone bill. In a 1986 interview with Burton Hatlen, King's former English professor at the University of Maine informed me that King's "perception of women and motherhood owes much to his life with Tabby. She continues to educate him, and her influence is apparent in the evolving presence of his women characters."

    I mention these biographical facts not from an effort to predispose King's audience to my understanding of his fiction, nor as an attempt to posit a Freudian interpretation of the artist's work, but merely to supply the reader with a deeper appreciation of the source where the central and recurring elements in King's novels and tales may indeed have originated.

Chapter 7
Giving Birth to Salvation:
The Mystery of Motherhood

"I have seen men leave the delivery room white and tottering and I have seen them swoon like girls, overcome by the cries and the blood."
--Stella Flanders, "The Reach"

At the International Popular Culture Association's 1987 meeting in Montreal, Canada, there were two separate groups of papers devoted to the fiction of Stephen King. In conversation that followed the presentation of articles in one of the sessions, the topic of King's fictional treatment of minorities--particularly blacks and women--was raised by several members of the audience. The general sentiment of those participating in the discussion was that although King tries to be favorably disposed toward both groups in fashionably liberal portraits, his characterizations of blacks and women lack substance.

One paper at the conference specifically addressed the issue of King's women. Jackie Eller's "Morality is the Message: Image-making of Female Characters in the Work of Stephen King," argued that King's restricted perspective as a male is evinced in the majority of female characters he has drawn. Eller could find no evidence of mature--much less powerful--women in King's canon.
Instead, she found only the many references to women as physical beings: King's sexist attention to lascivious anatomical details and the decadent evil of feminine sexuality. If King's blacks are strictly one-dimensional, less mortal than divine, devoid of the human contradictions and conflicts that are an engaging aspect of his white male protagonists, then his women, in Eller's view, suffer worse fates: instead of divine, they are either diabolical sorceresses or passive victims.

Eller's critical judgment is persuasive, and it certainly found sufficient support within the membership of her session's audience. As argued in an earlier chapter of this book, King's negative portraits of feminine sexuality represent a dominant motif in his fictional canon. But there exists another side to King's perception of women that, while perhaps not quite as glaring as his negative portrayals, is certainly more compelling to readers of both sexes.

On several notable occasions, King's women show themselves to be as strong as the supernatural forces they encounter and stronger than the men with whom they associate. Beverly Marsh in It and Dayna Jurgens in The Stand, for example, assert themselves against the violence that manifests itself in each respective book. In The Stand Dayna's refusal to provide Flagg with critical information about the Free Zone's spies shows a mental and moral toughness that is the equivalent of the dark man's own resolve. Moreover, her suicide is the first real moment in the novel where Flagg's dominion is directly challenged; her ability to thwart his interrogation highlights Flagg's essential weakness and foreshadows the eventual collapse of his empire. Dayna's act of defiance, as Lloyd realizes abruptly, is an indication of Flagg's vulnerability:

> "'I'll tell you something," Lloyd said, leaning forward. "He's losing his stuff. You ever hear that fucking saying? It's the eighth inning and he's losing his stuff and there's no-fucking-body warming up in the bullpen.
> . . . "Losing his stuff," Lloyd said, returning to his text. First Dayna, then this guy Cullen. His own wife--if that's what she was--goes and takes a dive. Do you think that was in his game plan?" (711-12)

Beverly Marsh is the only human female in It. We are initially introduced to her as a life-long victim of physical abuse from men--commencing with her father and extending to college boyfriends and her current husband. At the same time, however, this introduction also contains the seed for the more confident personality that she will establishin the course of the novel, as Beverly will discover alternatives to accepting passively the brutality of her own history.

In his attempt to keep her from going to

Derry, Beverly's husband, Tom, tries to administer yet another beating to re-assert control over his wife. For the first time in her life, Marsh rejects masculine authority, and in doing so she reconnects with the forceful identity she once possessed as an adolescent member of the Losers' Club:

> "If you come for me, I'm going to strap the shit out of you." The words were coming out of her mouth but she couldn't believe it was her saying them. And just who was this caveman in the bloody shorts, anyway? Her husband? Her father? The lover she had taken in college who had broken her nose one night, apparently on a whim? <u>Oh God help me</u>, she thought. <u>God help me now</u>. And still her mouth went on. "I can do it, too. You're fat and slow, Tom. I'm going, and I think maybe I'll stay gone. I think maybe it's over." (119)

When the Losers' Club must do battle against It, Beverly does not shrink from her male compatriots. In fact, quite the opposite, as she is the mystical center that holds the club together; first, by solidifying their union through sexual intercourse with each of the males when they were adolescents, and then later by providing Bill Denbrough and Ben Hanscomb with the determination to overcome their fears and confront It directly as adults. Although she, like all the other members of the Losers' Club, is technically childless, Marsh's protective dedication to each of the boy-men from her past marks her as the great earth mother in this novel, and her heroism is meant to serve as a counterforce to the sinister powers--and essential cowardice--of the female It.

Like Mother Abigail in <u>The Stand</u>, Beverly Marsh is a surrogate mother for each of the individuals struggling on the side of good. The moral centers of novels such as <u>The Shining</u>, <u>Cujo</u>, and <u>The Breathing Method</u> revolve around the special relationship that literally exists between a mother and her child. King's "simple" American wives and mothers--Wendy Torrance, Donna Trenton (<u>Cujo</u>), Franny Goldsmith (<u>The Stand</u>), and Stella

("The Reach")--are women not nearly so one-dimensional as Professor Eller purports. Each of these housewives may not be paragons of a radical feminist consciousness, but neither are they simpering nor passive. In final judgment, each of these women characters acts in a manner that is more courageous than their respective husbands or mates.

In *The Shining* and *Cujo* it is the devotion of a mother for her son that produces courageous action in both Wendy and Donna. While the fathers each adopt self-pitying postures and participate in acts of self-disintegration, willingly jeopardizing themselves and their children to hostile forces, the mothers struggle to assert control over environments that threaten their children and themselves. Donna Trenton's concern in her battle against the rabid Cujo is never for herself; her focus is always on preserving Tad by keeping him protected from the viciousness that surrounds them.

In *The Shining* Wendy Torrance emerges, at least as much as Hallorann, as the heroine of the book. As the Delbert Grady ghost points out to Jack after a particularly humiliating defeat at Wendy's hands, "'She appears to be . . . somewhat stronger than we had imagined. Somewhat more resourceful. She certainly seems to have gotten the better of you'" (381). While Jack's character becomes ever more circumscribed as a result of his obsession with the Overlook, Wendy actively rejects the hotel's domination: "She had never been tried in fire. Now the trial was upon her, not fire but ice, and she would not be allowed to sleep through this. Her son was waiting for her upstairs" (364). Like Donna Trenton, Wendy willfully places herself between Danny and the assorted specters that manifest themselves in her husband. As Wendy eventually concludes: "There are certain realities, as lunatic as this situation may seem. One of them is that you may be the only responsible person left in this grotesque pile. You have a five-going-on-six son to look out for" (366). While the father-husbands in these two novels retreat into the isolation of their own minds, the mother-wives come forth to command the same qualities of love and unselfish sacrifice that we have traced as the only avenues for moral endurance in King's fictional microcosm.

Courage and a profound commitment to the welfare of children are constants in King's descriptions of mothers throughout his canon. The level of responsibility that Donna Trenton and Wendy Torrance exert toward the welfare of their sons can likewise be found in King's portraits of expectant mothers as well.

In the novella *The Breathing Method* Emlyn McCarron explains the process of birth through the metaphor of a machine:

> "Birth is a wonderful thing, gentlemen, but I have never found it beautiful--not by any stretch of the imagination. I believe it is too brutal to be beautiful. A woman's womb is like an engine. With conception, that engine is turned on. At first it barely idles . . . but as the creative cycle nears the climax of birth, that engine revs up and up and up. Its idling whisper becomes a steady running hum, and then a rumble, and finally a bellowing, frightening roar. Once that engine has been turned on, every mother-to-be understands that her life is in check. Either she will bring the baby forth and the engine will shut down, or that engine will pound harder and louder and faster until it explodes, killing her in blood and pain." (462)

This "engine" within every woman is a powerful, frightening thing--a forcefulness that baffles men because they neither fully comprehend nor trust it. As we have seen in a preceeding chapter of this book, King's descriptions of feminine sexuality--Christine, the ghost woman at the Overlook, the affiliation between menstruation and telekinesis in Carrie White--are often indicative of an unfathomable destructive potential. Sexually, King suggests that the feminine engine is to be watched carefully, as it often "explodes, killing in blood and pain." But it is curious that while the writer maintains this misogynistic bias, he also endows his mothers and expectant mothers with a set of opposing values: a paradoxical capacity for selfless devotion that few of his male characters approximate.

In the novels and stories of Stephen King, mothers and pregnant women exhibit a degree of self-discipline that distinguishes them from the negative association between evil and feminine sexuality found elsewhere in his fiction. The principle that animates the mist in "Strawberry Spring" or the infernal machine in <u>Christine</u> is destructive because it relies upon manipulation in order to increase its own level of influence. The ghost-woman at the Overlook, for example, is only concerned with subsuming Danny Torrance's capacity to shine into herself, and to secure this end the hotel is willing to ensnare and then discard Danny's father. King frequently portrays feminine sexuality as dangerous because it serves only itself, or rather the evil that is just beneath the surface of its animation. Like the many examples of "masculine" evil in his fiction--Flagg, Greg Stillson (<u>The Dead Zone</u>), Richard Sloat--the author's characterizations of feminine sexuality are delineated by an absence of compassion and the urge to isolate and destroy.

The writer's mothers and mother-to-be, however, put their children before themselves. There exists a kind of mysteriousness to their response, but unlike the the ambiguous <u>femme fatales</u> in <u>The Shining</u> and <u>Christine</u>, King's pregnant women possess an air of majesty that reflects the miracle of birth itself. His maternal women invert Christine's formula of violence leading to weakness and death, to violence leading to power and life.

In <u>The Breathing Method</u> Sandra Stansfield is an expectant mother. She is a single woman, deserted by the man who impregnated her, and left to face the demeaning, unaccepting world she lives in on her own. In the historical setting which serves as a backdrop for the tale, society has no pretensions to liberal thought regarding women who are in trouble: "'An unmarried pregnant woman was a trollop in the eyes of the world'" (465). Consequently, she eventually loses her job and is forced to find another place to live, but these setbacks do not deter her. She will do anything necessary to have and keep her baby, even if it means compromising her own principles:

"Sometimes I think the worst of this--of everything that's happened--is that it's changed the way I look at people. Sometimes I think to myself, 'How can you sleep at night knowing you've deceived that dear old thing?' and then I think, 'If she knew, she'd show you the door, just like all the others'. Either way it's a lie, and I feel the weight of it on my heart sometimes . . . . 'I bought it [a ring] at a pawnshop,' she said 'For two dollars. And it's the only time during this whole nightmare that I've felt ashamed and dirty.'" (480, 485)

Sandra has been forced by society to make several very difficult choices; but in each case she chooses what will make life best for her baby. If she must lie, she will, but she does not enjoy doing so. She is a victim of a hypocritical and judgmental world. Yet McCarron gives a clear picture of a woman who is nonetheless in control of her life, a woman who knows what she wants and will eventually get it. Sandra has learned to depend upon herself, and the reader sees that she has attained a level of dignity from her struggle. She accepts her responsibilities with grace, bravery, and without shame:

"She had not engaged in the usual shilly-shallying, toe-scuffing, blushing, tearful behavior. She had been straight-forward and businesslike. Even her alias seemed more like a matter of business than a matter of shame... 'but rather than trusting to the professional ethics of a man I don't know, I'll trust in myself. If you don't mind' . . . . She was merely an extremely serious, extremely determined young woman . . . . She had guts. All kinds of guts. One couldn't deny that.... I liked the way she was handling a problem that would have reduced ninety women out of hundred into inept and undignified liars." (463-69)

But just as Sandra Stansfield is unable to control her society's condemnation of her condition, she likewise senses an air of impending disaster: "'I have a feeling, Dr. McCarron, sometimes a quite strong feeling, that I am doomed'" (484). This air of tragic resignation strengthens Sandra as a character; she doesn't run away from her situation or deny its reality in any manner. Even with the odds so severely stacked against mother and child, her maternal instincts prevail against a callous fate.

On the evening Stansfield delivers her baby, she is involved in an accident which leaves her decapitated. Her head is severed from her body, yet she still maintains control over her torso, continuing fastidiously with the breathing exercises she has practiced in preparation for birth. She should, by all scientific evidence, be dead, but her concentration allows her to hold on long enough to bear the child she loves so deeply. She lives to hear that she has delivered a boy. Stansfield exhibits a determination and courage that surpasses what is thought to be humanly possible. She may not be able to control her fate, but she is able to accomplish her quest. Her baby lives and out of the mother's death comes new life. She does not die in vain, but with dignity and a sense of accomplishment.

In <u>The Stand</u> we are presented several women who resemble Sandra Stansfield's attributes of discipline and determination. Frannie, Lucy, and Nadine Cross all conceive children during the course of the novel. All three of them live in a desolate, foreign land, the remains of civilization threatened by an evil force from the West. Their world is unstable and frightening; all three of them are basically alone. And each in her own way is courageous and strong.

Frannie Goldsmith, one of the main characters of this novel, is the only one to conceive before the superflu arrives. The father of her baby succumbs to the flu, and although she later will find a friend and lover in Stu Redman, she is without a partner when it is time for her to give birth.

Early in the book when her father dies, rather than let herself lapse into impotent grief, Frannie summons the will to bury him: "'Who's going to bury him?' And at the sound of her own voice, the answer came. It was perfectly clear. She was, of course. Who else? She was" (153). She is clearly a young woman who can accept responsibility for what she must do. Unlike the biological father of her child, Jessie, Frannie does not flee the consequences of her actions. Like Wendy Torrance and Donna Trenton, her first priority is to the people she loves, especially her baby. Every thought she has concerns his welfare, and the fact that she must continually endure the uncertainty of his immunity to the superflu strengthens her resolve and deepens her personality. When nightmares about the dark man require the other Free Zone citizens to resort to mild tranquilizers in order to sleep through the night, she chooses to suffer through the dreams rather than risk damage to her fetus. She also keeps a diary so that if her child lives it will know what the world had been like before the plague. In contrast to Harold Lauder's personal journal, which is strictly a self-referential document filled with hate, Frannie writes for and about others: "In a way she was keeping it [the diary] for the baby. It was an act of faith-- faith that the baby would live" (348).

Her dedication is all the more remarkable in light of the dark man's attempts to intimidate her. She dreams of what he would do to her baby:

> In the dream she was climbing the stairs again, going to her father, to do her duty... It wasn't her father under there. And what was under there was not dead. Something-- someone--filled with dark life and hideous good cheer was under there . . . he was grinning, but she couldn't see his face. Aware of the frigid cold blasting up at her from that awful grin. No, she couldn't see his face, but she could see the gift this terrible man had brought for her unborn child: a twisted coathanger. (159-60)

Flagg does not get her baby, and neither does the superflu. The child survives and becomes a symbol of hope in a world filled with despair. Unlike Sandra, however, Frannie likewise survives and is able to nurture her young son and watch him grow. At the conclusion of *The Stand*, Frannie remains a survivor; she has regained a sense of balance in this chaotic landscape by re-establishing a familial relationship with her children and husband. Her new family, although cognizant of the tragedies they have witnessed and the uncertainty still ahead of them, is the single most optimistic product of the Free Zone.

Other pregnant women in *The Stand* share with Frannie and Sandra the strength and bravery that makes them unique. Both Lucy and Nadine go through their pregnancies virtually alone. They inhabit the same hostile, volatile world that Frannie does. Lucy shares with Frannie the fear that her babies will not survive because of the superflu.

Nadine's fear, on the other hand, is that her baby will survive. It is this possibility that makes her reject Flagg. Although she spends the better part of the novel waiting for him to call for her, saving her virginity for him, once she is impregnated with the realization that she is to bring his child into the world, she hardens herself against him.

> His hands slammed down on her shoulders, snapping both collarbones like pencils. He lifted her bodily high over his head into the faded blue desert sky, as he pivoted on his heels he threw her, up and out, as he had thrown the glass. He saw the great smile of relief and triumph on her face, the sudden sanity in her eyes, and understood. She had baited him into doing it, understanding somehow that only he could set her free--and she was carrying his child. (702)

Nadine finds freedom in death; she has saved the world from the demon-child that she would have borne. Significantly, it is her pregnancy which instills her with the resolve to dismiss Flagg, a purposefulness and clarity of insight that Nadine lacked until she was on the verge of motherhood. Her last moments emphasize her sanity and relief. Like Sandra, her death means something: Her final act is one of unselfishness toward others, even if that altruism requires her to destroy her own child. For Nadine's decision to die actually shows evidence of a commitment to her child. She knows that life as the progeny of a fiend as evil as Flagg would be absent of joy and goodness. The child would know only anguish. To bring the offspring of Flagg into an already unstable world, would only mean more destruction and despair, and Nadine knows that she is responsible for producing a good measure of the suffering herself.

In contrast to Nadine, Lucy lives, and so do her babies, twins, who join Frannie's child as symbols of hope and renewal for the post-holocaust world into which they are born. These women have lived through a nightmare, and have awakened to a bright future. In fact, their children represent this future: the chance to avoid making the same mistakes that produced the superflu's devastation. Motherhood gives both Lucy and Frannie the will to survive--and they have done so.

Sandra, Nadine, Lucy and Frannie are all women with stong characters and firm resolutions. They are women the reader cannot help but admire. They find themselves in the worst of all possible circumstances and they deal with their situations like mature, responsible adults. They accept their individual fates and make the best of them. They are selfless and firm in their commitments, both to their children and the world into which they bring them.

There is no doubt that King means to make these women special, and that part of their uniqueness emerges from their states of pregnancy. It is as if McCarron's engine metaphor sparks more than merely a physical change; it supplies these women with an interior strength as well, a moral resolve. Unlike the self-serving (and ultimately self-destructive) references to feminine sexuality throughout works as diverse as Christine, Carrie, and "Strawberry Spring," King's pregnant women share loving bonds with other human beings. This connection provides these women with qualities and resourcefulness that men will never have and will never truly understand. McCarron's final recollection of Sandra Stansfield reflects the outsider's point of view: "She considered me briefly and then smiled--a secret smile which I am convinced only pregnant women know" (468).

Stephen King, like most honest males, senses the mystery associated with motherhood; he holds pregnant women in a sort of religious awe. They are a true mystery--Madonna-like--but all of them are also created out of flesh and blood rather than an abstract principle. At the Popular Culture Conference mentioned at the beginning of this chapter, Burton Hatlen, King's friend and former college professor from the University of Maine, argued that Tabitha King, Steve's wife, continues to exert a tremendous influence on shaping her husband's attitude toward women, and that the evolving presence of King's female characters owes much to his relationship with a feminist wife. It would seem a likely corollary that the three children who represent the fruits of this marriage have done much to ennoble the role of motherhood in Stephen King's mind.

King's positive treatment of motherhood notwithstanding, there are, finally, painfully few examples of "independant women" in his canon. Those who do live alone, without children and/or husbands, appear particularly susceptible to the extreme perversions and psychologically unstable behavior of Annie Wilkes in <u>Misery</u>. The reader may recall that Annie abandons her life-long murder spree only for the duration of her marriage, and that her divorce increases the frequency and wantonness of her psychotic acts. Even King's strong madonna figures continue to support the traditional premise that in a man's world women are free only in order to give themselves to their children. At least at this point in his literary career, motherhood remains the only avenue available to King's women which allows them to express a level of determination and power equal to or greater than a man's.

With the notable exception of Nadine Cross, the female characters examined in this chapter are a moral, straightforward group of people. They don't steal other women's husbands or boyfriends, suffer from major neuroses or psychoses, tell lies, or engage in manipulative behavior. Most of all, they are selflessly devoted to their children. Just as the madonna has always been at the opposite extreme from the whore in the exclusive view of patriachical culture, King's perception of women is a reflection of this bias. Once his women characters are removed from the realm of a wanton sexuality and placed into the responsibilities of motherhood, their allegiances can be seen to shift across the moral spectrum: from the ethical vacuum of a Christine Hargenson

(<u>Carrie</u>) at one end, to the saintly demeanor of Mother Abigail at the other. In short, as King's boys and men discover their nexus to moral salvation in male-bonding and his writer-artists through exercising their creative talents, King's women uncover its closest approximation in the maternal-child relationship. Sandra Stansfield's acknowledgment to Dr. McCarron just before her death in <u>The Breathing Method</u> stands as a maxim for all of King's moral voyagers, male and female alike: "'There's no salvation without suffering. It's a cheap magic, but it's all we have'" (485).

Chapter 8
Portraits of the Artist:
The Writer as Survivor

"If you are a real artist, you give your whole being to your art. Anything short of that, then you are not an artist."
--Miranda's journal,
John Fowles' The Collector, 134

There is little point in disputing the fact that much of Stephen King's popular appeal during the past decade has centered upon the fantastic occurrences which take place in his fiction. His writing is, no less than Tolkein or Lewis, often centered around magical events. But the magical in Stephen King's fiction appears in a wide variety of forms--exists, finally, in even more variations than we find in his two aforementioned fantasy predecessors. In King's world, the inanimate is animate ("Trucks," The Shining, and Christine); classic monsters from myth and folklore are resurrected ('Salem's Lot, It, Cycle of the Werewolf); new worlds issue forth (The Stand and The Talisman); and individuals possess special, supernatural powers of destruction and/or omniscience (Carrie, Firestarter, The Dead Zone). Some of these creations are borrowed from earlier conventions of gothic fiction, and are placed in a modern American context; others belong exclusively to King's own haunted psyche.

The magical in King's world, however, is not simply limited to the domain of supernatural events. Several of King's protagonists are writers, perhaps autobiographical reflections of the author himself, but nonetheless always in possession of certain powers of transcendence, talismanic qualities that are directly related to their occupation. Ben Mears in 'Salem's Lot, Gordie Lachance in The Body, Mike Hanlon and Bill Denbrough in It and Paul Sheldon in Misery are the most notable examples of the writer in King's canon. All of these males are distinguished from other characters by virtue of being artists: they possess insights and imaginative capabilities which, although not as dramatic as Danny Torrance's shine or Carrie White's telekinesis, are just as volatile and magical. The writer in

King's fiction occupies a role similar to the position the poet once held in ancient Greece and Rome: he is the keeper of moral tradition, the high elder who reasserts order in the midst of worldly chaos and destruction. While he may not possess supernatural abilities per se, he does possess powers to create and control.

Discussing the role of the artist in The Body, Leonard Heldreth posits that "writing succeeds for Gordon because it offers control over experience . . . . Writing permits a systematic formulation of the plan or world view and provides the means for keeping it before not only the author but all of his readers" (72-73). The writer's understanding of history, his sense of self-discipline, and his insights into humanity provide him with the potential for surviving the violence and depravity associated with evil, against which he is always pitted. The writer-protagonist in King's fiction is a hero; his craft supplies him with the prerequisite honesty and courage which he must use to combat evil's sophistries.

The careful reader of King's canon might be tempted to wonder where Jack Torrance fits into this scheme in his own capacity as a writer. Surely Jack's dedication to his craft is as strong as any of the other authors found elsewhere in King's fiction--why then does his art fail to insulate him against the residing powers at the Overlook? The obvious answer to this question is that Jack gives up on his writing at the very moment in which he needs it the most. It is possible to trace this gradual process of discouragement through the course of the novel. Early in The Shining Jack's commitment to his work is largely responsible for him regaining a measure of control over his alcoholism and quick temper. We learn this from both Jack and Wendy:

> The actual act of his writing made her immensely hopeful, not because she expected great things from the play but because her husband seemed to be slowly closing a huge door on a roomful of monsters. He had had his shoulder to that door for a long time now, but at last it was swinging shut. (121)

His desire to finish the play he is writing is the reason the caretaker position at the Overlook appeals to him. Moreover, Al Shockley assures him that "'if that play comes to something'" it may help persuade the board to reinstate Jack to his former teaching position at Stovington (43). Thus, during his early residency at the Overlook, before his discovery of the cardboard box and scrapbook containing past records of the hotel itself, the play is Jack's primary motivation in life, and his only source of real anticipation. The Overlook, however, wants to redirect Jack's energies away from the play and toward himself, essentially reopening "the huge door" that barely restrains the "roomful of monsters" inhabiting Jack's own psyche. In its systematic intrusion into Jack's identity, one of the first things the Overlook takes from him is his art. By drawing attention away from work on his play, in order to refocus it on the history of the hotel itself, the demons at the Overlook essentially separate Jack from his writing. Director Stanley Kubrick seems to sense the importance of this development in the film version of The Shining: the sheets of paper all mindlessly repeating the same carefully typed sentence--"All work and no play makes Jack a dull boy"--are meant to illustrate the dissolution of Torrance's skill and artistic dedication. Consequently, by the final third of the novel, Jack is no longer even interested in his writing, much less pursuing the completion of his play. He gradually abandons his work until all references to it disappear from the text completely. His artistic dedication slowly erodes as Jack changes occupations from writer to eternal caretaker of the hotel. By the end of the novel he identifies wholly with the destructive spirit that animates the Overlook. And his sense of commitment to the responsibilit. that are associated with his former self--father, husband, writer--are surrendered unconditionally. It is not accidental, then, that Jack's loss of his craft parallels the abrogation of his mind and spirit to the Overlook.

In contrast to Jack Torrance, whose literary skills depreciate in the course of his stay at the Overlook, Bill Denbrough in It develops his artistic attributes and employs them in face-to-face battle against the sewer monster, It. The Ritual of Chud is a sort of linguistical contest between monster and man, and it is fitting that Denbrough, himself a highly successful and productive writer of horror fiction, is the representative from the Loser's Club. Denbrough is the "soul" of the Losers' Club: he is their natural leader who has suffered more than others (his brother, George, is killed by It and Bill feels the guilt of responsibility), and who possesses, because of his role as writer, a keen awareness of moral absolutes and the importance of maintaining them. This is one explanation for It's fear of him; Bill's mental prowess enabled him to vanquish the monster twenty- seven years ago. It knows that "<u>The writer was the strongest, the one who had somehow trained his mind for this confrontation over all the years, and when the writer was dead with his guts falling out of his body, when their precious 'Big Bill' was dead, the others would be Its quickly</u>" (1018).

In <u>Danse Macabre</u> King asserts that

> The imagination is an eye, a marvelous third eye that floats free. As children that eye sees with 20/20 clarity. As we grow older, its vision begins to dim... The job of the fantasy writer, or the horror writer, is to bust the walls of that tunnel vision wide for a little while; to provide a single powerful spectacle for that third eye. The job of the fantasy-horror writer is to make you, for a little while, a child again. (378)

As a writer of horror novels, Bill's imagination is fueled by his fiction, so that he not only makes his readers children again, but is likewise capable of reinvigorating himself through his art. He recognizes that his own history and Derry's are inexorably linked, so that the stories he has written as an adult are not only inspired by his childhood, but also connect to his life as a grown-up. Bill leads the charge against It because he has a personal debt to repay in avenging his brother's death. In fact, it is clear that his own sense of guilt over the loss of his brother (he feels somehow responsible for the boy's death) finds its only relief in the act of writing horror fiction. His memory of this event, as Audra tells him just before making the trip from England to Maine, "'has cast a shadow over [his] dreams'" (134).

Like the other members of the Losers' Club, Denbrough cannot remember exactly the events that transpired twenty-seven years ago. But to vanquish It forever, he needs to recreate the Ritual of Chüd. His skill as a writer helps in this quest, as a novelist's obsession is with the past, "'these memories waiting to be born'" (140). In order to produce his art, the artist must be willing to face his memories honestly and without flinching--this active struggle is his only hope for gaining control over them. Thus, to destroy It, Denbrough the adult discovers nothing short of a magical conduit to Denbrough the child. This process turns out to be easier than Bill anticipated, since his job as a writer has helped him to maintain "a single powerful spectacle for that third eye."

> They struck together with their right fists but Bill understood it was not really their fists they were striking with at all; it was their combined force, augmented by the force of that Other; it was the force of memory and desire; above all else, it was the force of love and unforgotten childhood like one big wheel . . . .
> You don't have to look back to see those children; part of your mind will see them forever, love with them forever. They are not necessarily the best part of you, but they were once the repository of all you could become. (1092, 1135)

Bill Denbrough is the definitive authorial presence in this novel: the book begins with his reflections on the death of his brother and ends with his rescue of Audra, as the latter is reborn from a catatonic coma. His artistic imagination allows Bill to come full circle: from a state of impotence when he loses his brother to It, to a state of magical empowerment as he brings Audra back to consciousness.

But Bill is not the only writer in _It_ who relies upon his imaginative powers to construct a pipeline that connects two realms of chronological time. Mike Hanlon's journal entries likewise open a corridor to his own past--to his father and childhood. It is a result of the introspective journey afforded by his journal writing that Hanlon gains the insight and courage to recognize the current seriousness of the situation in Derry and to summon the members of the Losers' Club for a final confrontation with It. Through the use of his journal, in the act of remembering history by writing it down, Hanlon comes to associate the "accidental disappearances" of Derry's children in 1985 to other similar incidents from the town's sordid past. The recurring shadow of Pennywise the clown extends beyond current Derry curfews and back into the dim recollections of Hanlon's childhood. His journal gives these memories illumination.

But even more important than recognizing the need to signal his friends to return to Maine, Hanlon's writing reminds Mike of his father's bravery in the face of Derry's tradition of violence and cruelty. Recalling his father's precedent instills a similar resolve in Mike; the history that is recorded in his journal is not merely a record of Pennywise's wanton evil, it also contains the memory of individual acts of endurance and defiance in the face of this evil. The evidence of black men struggling against the racist power structures of Derry parallels the Losers' Club's quest against It. Indeed, Mike's father and friends unconsciously serve as models of inspiration for Mike and his friends.

Against Derry's moral disintegration, for example, is Dick Hallorann's willingness to sacrifice himself to save the lives of others on the night the Black Spot is torched. Like the blacks who found the night club in flagrant rejection of Derry's atmosphere of racial oppression, Mike Hanlon, a generation later, refuses to condone the town's subtle attempts to cover-up the disappearance of its children. Hanlon's journal becomes a microcosmic mirror to King's own stylistic endeavor throughout the novel to juxtapose past with present until the two time sequences are inseparable. The town's history of racism, Mike's own childhood memories of the bird that attacked him, and the current situation in Derry are drawn together in the pages of Mike's journal:

> I wrote until long after three this morning, pushing the pen faster and faster, trying to get it all out. I had forgotten about seeing the giant bird when I was eleven. It was my father's story that brought it back . . . and I suppose it was his final gift to me. A terrible gift, you might say, but wonderful in its way. (470-1)

As we have seen in the character of Bill Denbrough, memory is a gift for Mike Hanlon as well because it inspires him to initiate action against It. King's author-protagonists find themselves in positions that force them to analyze the past, and from this activity they uncover a private, personal strength. In the process these characters find themselves largely separated from other men by virtue of their professional insights, but this social distance is really a blessing, as it allows them to eschew social conformity. Like the incidents of male-bonding that occur elsewhere in King's canon, his writers are free to create their own destinies. Their moral journeys inevitably lead them away from the corruption they encounter in society and toward states of purification. Unlike the citizens of 'Salem's Lot, whose transformation into vampires reflect, in Douglas Winter's words, "the seductiveness of evil and the dehumanizing pall of modern society," (37) Ben Mears's role as a writer forces him to confront the secret of the town by acknowledging its essential corruption. Whereas the other members of this community, like the adults in Derry, refuse to recognize the spiritual depravity of their town, Mears takes action against the immorality he uncovers. Mears is motivated, like Denbrough and Hanlon, by an intrinsic moral purpose that at once alienates and elevates him from the other inhabitants of 'Salem's Lot. His survival takes place because he rejects the evil that is besetting the town. Indeed, the fire he starts that consumes the entire city is the flame of purification, and it stands as an individual challenge to an entire community's moral disintegration.

Even as he is drawn to the lure of Barlow, Mears, unlike Father Callahan, keeps his faith in himself. This self-insulation is born from the very courage that brings the author back to the town of his childhood in order to face (by writing about them) the fears that have troubled him since adolescence. By confronting these fears on paper, Mears learns how to confront and conquer others that await him in real life; his writing is nothing less than an act of self-empowerment.

Stephen King's 1987 novel <u>Misery</u> begins and ends inside a writer's imagination. Paul Sheldon, a famous American author of historical romances, spends virtually the entire book as the captive of a psychopathic nurse. Annie Wilkes has kidnapped her "favorite writer" after a crippling car accident. Although she has rescued him from the winter's cold, his legs are reduced to mangled bone and cartilage. Moreover, he is addicted to the drugs she employs as a method for controlling his excruciating pain.

But it is always more than merely his physical survival that fascinates Nurse Wilkes; like the Ferdinand-Caliban character in John Fowles' novel <u>The Collector</u>--clearly King's primary influence in the writing of <u>Misery</u>--Annie desires to <u>know</u> her subject, to possess it in a way that resembles Caliban's obsession with butterflies and beautiful women: "She really was an idol, and if she didn't kill him, she might kill what was <u>in</u> him" (26). One of the more engaging aspects of Fowles' novel is that the complex Caliban is at once attracted to and frightened by his female captive. Extraordinarily unsure of himself in Miranda's presence, Caliban fluctuates between adoration and violent disgust. Annie Wilkes is also capable of similar mood swings, one minute telling Paul how much she loves him, the next dispassionately severing his foot with an axe and blowtorch. Both Caliban and Annie are sexually repressed individuals, opposed to profanity of any sort, yet their quaint, cliche-riddled language and postures barely mask an undercurrent of aggression that threatens to overwhelm them at any moment:

> The climate inside her, he had come to discover, was like spring-time in the Midwest. She was a woman full of tornadoes waiting to happen, and if he had been a farmer observing a sky which looked the way Annie's face looked right now, he would have at once gone to collect his family and herd them into the storm cellar. (64)

Unable to escape from the hospitality of their captors, Fowles' Miranda and King's Sheldon retreat into their respective artistic imaginations. But where Caliban recognizes that he will never fully understand Miranda's paintings or her love of art (his confusion and ignorance, which are always bordering on the edge of fear, produces some of their greatest moments of miscommunication), Annie is intrigued at the prospect of following Paul into the creation of a new novel.

From her introduction on the second page of the novel, forcing breath into his feeble body "the way a man might force a part of himself into an unwilling woman," (4) Annie remains in control of Paul's physical life. That domination, however, is merely a prelude to a more intimate and personal violation. She rapes him throughout the book by insisting that he use his craft to bring back Misery, Annie's favorite fictional heroine who died in Sheldon's latest romance. She is a kind of psychic vampire, sucking Paul's inspiration and creativity in order to fashion a world according to Wilkes. Just as her rural farmhouse, complete with disconnected telephone and other warped attempts at normality, mirrors her paranoid mental condition, she means to have her favorite author create a fictional realm exactly to her specifications. As long as the writer cooperates, Annie will exercise some restraint over her psychopathic tendencies, assuring him, for example, that he will live long enough to finish the novel.

Paul's writing, then, becomes at once both a release from the madness of Annie Wilkes and another kind of bondage, as his fiction must please his "number one fan"--his life depends upon it. Like Miranda's own identification with Caliban's elaborate butterfly collection in <u>The Collector</u>, "'all the beauty you've ended,'" (52) Paul makes a similar personal connection to a childhood memory of a caged exotic bird from Africa:

> An awful memory bloomed there in the dark: his mother had taken him to the Boston Zoo, and he had been looking at a great big bird. It had the most beautiful feathers--red and purple and royal blue--that he had ever seen . . . and the saddest eyes. He had asked his mother where the bird came from and when she said <u>Africa</u> he had understood it was doomed to die in the cage where it lived, far away from whatever God had meant it to be, and he cried and his mother bought him an ice-cream cone and for awhile he had stopped crying and then he remembered and started again and so she had taken him home, telling him as they rode the trolley back to Lynn that he was a bawl-baby and a sissy. (27)

The bird is, of course, a metaphor for Paul's state of entrapment--tortured and abandoned, uprooted from his past against his will--but unlike the caged bird, Paul refuses to accept passively his role as victim. To an extent even greater than Miranda's rebellion in <u>The Collector</u>, he learns that the creative process can also be a weapon, a momentary stay against the forces of confusion, to paraphrase Robert Frost's definition of poetry. In summoning his authorial voice, Paul realizes for the first time that an artist possesses strength as great as any cage that is employed to restrain him:

> Yet something in her attitude as she stood in the doorway fascinated him. It was as if she was a little frightened to come any closer--as if she thought something in him might burn her . . . . The furnace was on. Oh, not that he had written particularly well--the story was hot, but the characters as stereotyped and predictable as ever--but this time he had been able to at least generate some power; this time there was heat baking out from between

the lines.

Amused, he thought: <u>She felt the heat. I think she's afraid to get too close in case I might burn her</u>. (137)

While Annie's tyranny brings to the surface all of Sheldon's self-doubts about the true quality of his art (he knows that his fame and fortune have been purchased by writing second-rate fiction), it also issues a challenge to this self to prove once and for all that he deserves to make a living (and to continue living) through the magic of words:

<u>Yeah. You bet I can. There's a million things in this world I can't do. Couldn't hit a curve ball, even back in high school. Can't fix a leaky faucet. Can't roller-skate or make an F-chord on the guitar that sounds like anything but shit. I have tried to be married and couldn't do it either time. But if you want me to take you away, to scare you or involve you or make you cry or grin, yeah. I can. I can bring it to you and keep bringing it until you holler uncle. I am able. I CAN.</u> (108)

This is where Paul's only authority is found. Just as any good writer holds his audience in captivity for the length of a narrative, suspended from everyday concerns in a landscape of the author's own making, Paul uses his confinement to write the best Misery novel of his career.

The reawakening of Paul's imaginative talents also rekindles his will to live and to escape from Annie's bondage. It likewise resuscitates his moral capacities insofar as his own captivity forges a bond of sympathy and anger that extends beyond himself. When Wilkes leaves him for days in order to go off to her "Laughing Place," Paul's own suffering opens him to the anguish of the abandoned animals in Annie's barn. Like the exotic bird from Africa, they are all victims of a wanton human cruelty:

He was a little surprised at the depth of sympathy he felt for the animals and the depth of anger at Annie for how she had, in her unadmitting and arrogant egotism, left them to suffer in their pens.

> If your animals could talk, Annie, they would tell you who the REAL dirty birdie around here is. (187)

The production of Paul's novel, Misery's Return, parallels his life as Annie's captive: the writer is kept alive only because Annie remains obsessed with "the power of the gotta," (230) the need to discover what will happen next in the narrative. The writing, on the other hand, while initially Paul's only card in a deck stacked against him, grows to become his conduit to survival. Although Sheldon never really asserts absolute control over the situation until he ends up killing Annie, he steadily gains the ability to exert leverage over her psychosis: " . . . I had a certain passive hold over her" (230). It is, moreover, the discipline that he has cultivated as a writer that keeps him from further punishments as a result of lashing out at Annie or making any attempt to overpower her physically until he is in a position to do so successfully. In contrast to Annie's volatile personality, Paul's self-control keeps him focused on survival and life. She, on the other hand, is beyond self-government, even more addicted to her "fictional fix" than Sheldon is to the Norvil.

When her "pet writer" apparently burns the complete manuscript of Misery's Return before she reads its conclusion, Annie loses final control over an environment that began to change the afternoon she presented Paul with a typewriter. Thus, it is only slightly ironic that this same typewriter, initially a further torment to Paul as he must compose Misery's Return upon it, should become the weapon that literally produces Annie's death when she trips over it:

> She had actually died of the fractured skull she had received when she had struck the mantel, and she had struck the mantel because she had tripped. So in a way she had been killed by the very typewriter Paul had hated so much. (307)

At the conclusion of <u>Misery</u>, Paul's misery is a recurring series of Annie Wilkes hallucinations: he sees her in the alleys of New York, in the shadows of his apartment, at the end of dark corridors. His paranoia indicates that he is still healing from the mental scars of his imprisonment, even as his body has nearly fully recuperated. And in his lonely suffering, Paul reconnects to the only certainty that ever existed in his life: the stability that is born "through the hole in the page" in the act of writing. By commencing a new novel, the Annie memories are held at bay. Her Novril capsules were never as effective:

> He could. He <u>could</u>.
> So, in gratitude and in terror, he <u>did</u>. The hole opened and Paul stared through at what was there, unaware that his fingers were picking up speed, unaware that his legs were in the same city but fifty blocks away, unaware that he was weeping as he wrote. (310)

More than ultimately thwarting Annie's powers of intimidation, returning to his art, to the creative process, to the old Paul Sheldon, is final affirmation of his willingness and ability to regain control over himself. The very skills required to be a real artist are also what is necessary to endure the Nietzschian abyss that King quotes as the prologue to Part I.

The chaos and darkness that threaten modern man's identity and moral survival occupy a variety of shapes in King's fiction: vampires in a small Maine town, a creature that haunts an urban sewer system, a hotel with a long history of depravity, or a psychotic Colorado farm woman. Annie Wilkes is an image of the great perverse Bourkas goddess that torments Misery in <u>Misery's</u> <u>Return</u>. But Paul's humanity and his stubborn refusal to surrender to Annie's despair keep him from sacrificing either his new book or his mind at the altar of this insane idol in a nurse's uniform. Even at the climax of the novel, after experiencing the full range of Annie's psychosis, Paul is still capable of separating himself from the nihilism of her world-view. Recalling both

Miranda's dignity and compassion in the midst of her own nightmare in The Collector, Paul is likewise able to render an objective, even sympathetic response to his tormentor:

> Paul thought that the occasional moments like this were the most gastly of all, because in them he saw the woman she might have been if her upbringing had been right or the drugs squirted out by all the funny little glands inside her had been less wrong. Or both. (282)

Out of his self-discipline and mental toughness, but most of all from the inspiration afforded by his writing talents, Paul Sheldon maintains his balance as he crawls along the perimeter of the abyss. Like any successful artistic endeavor, his journey shows him how to create meaning out of personal suffering, triumph out of despair. Although he will never walk normally again, having lost both a foot and a thumb to his surgical nurse, Sheldon emerges from his ordeal a more complete human being than when he began it.

A writer creates his own reality through the manipulation of language. There is the potential for profound egotism in this, yet each of the characters we have considered in this chapter is an altruistic man. King's writer-protagonists make their lives their craft, but they also owe their lives to their craft. The art--the skill of writing--is real magic, and the individual man who utilizes it must also stand in awe of it. This magic remains so intoxicating that the personal identities of King's writers cannot be separated from their art. Even as Paul Sheldon anticipates working at Annie Wilkes' Royal typewriter with a profound dread, once he has begun composing Misery's Return he could no more break the incantation than jog back to Denver.

Moral survival in King's fiction--whether it be in the form of male-bonding, an artist's confrontation with himself, or, in a mother's love for her child-- comes from within the individual. In tapping into this reserve, the self is in turn deepened and enlarged. The power of the written word is talismanic in King's world: it is a means for his characters to regain control over their own lives and the lives of those who touch them. In this sense, King inverts the cliched romantic exultation of art being the product of madness (or at least, like Poe's Roderick Usher, the notion of art and madness as a reflection of one another). Instead, King offers the means to salvation through art: the dark chaos of the world can be managed, but only through the illumination of a mind that has labored to gain control over itself. As King reminds us in <u>Danse Macabre</u>, "Fiction is the truth inside the lie, and in the tale of horror as in any other tale, the same rule applies now as when Aristophanes told his horror tale of the frogs: morality is telling the truth as your heart knows it" (375). The writer's illuminating magic of liberation, in contrast to evil's dark magic of oppression, is the transcendent gift that emerges from a cultivated level of self-discipline and honest self-examination. If there is a strength to be found in staring into the abyss, King hastens to inform us that even greater power is to be had in the act of writing about it.

WORKS CITED

Bettelheim, Bruno. *The Uses of Enchantment: The Meaning and Importance of Fairy Tales*. New York: Viking, 1977.

Collings, Michael. *The Many Facets of Stephen King*. Mercer Island, WA: Starmont House, 1985.

_____ and David Engebretson. *The Shorter Works of Stephen King*. Mercer Island, WA: Starmont House, 1985.

Cook, Reginald. "The Forest of Young Goodman Brown's Night: A Reading of Hawthorne's 'Young Goodman Brown.'" *New England Quarterly* 43 (1970): 473-481.

Deamer, Robert Glen. "Hawthorne's Dream in the Forest." *Western American Literature* 13 (1979): 327-340.

Eller, Jackie. "Morality is the Message: Image-making of Female Characters in the Work of Stephen King." Paper presented at the Popular Culture Association Meeting, Montreal, Canada, 29 March, 1987.

Fiedler, Leslie A. *Love and Death in the American Novel*. New York: Stein and Day, 1966.

Fowles, John. *The Collector*. New York: Del, 1963.

Hatlen, Burton. "Beyond the Kittery Bridge: Stephen King's Maine" in *Fear Itself*. Eds. Tim Underwood and Chuck Miller. New York: New American Library, 1986.

Hawthorne, Nathaniel. *The Celestial Railroad and Other Stories*. New York: New American Library, 1963.

Hawthorne, Nathaniel. *The Scarlet Letter*. New York: New American Library, 1959.

Heldreth, Leonard. "Viewing <u>The Body</u>: King's Portrait of the Artist as Survivor" in <u>The Gothic World of Stephen King: Landscape of Nightmares</u>. Eds. Gary Hoppenstand and Ray Browne. Bowling Green, OH: Bowling Green State University Popular Press, 1987.

Herron, Donald. "Horror Springs in the Fiction of Stephen King" in <u>Fear Itself</u>. Eds. Tim Underwood and Chuck Miller. New York: New American Library, 1985.

_____. "The Biggest Horror Fan of Them All" in <u>Discovering Stephen King</u>. Ed. Darrell Schweitzer. Mercer Island, WA: Starmont House, 1985..

Indick, Ben P.. "What Makes Him So Scary" in <u>Discovering Stephen King</u>. Ed. Darrell Schweitzer. Mercer Island, WA: Starmont House, 1985.

Keats, John. "La Belle Dame Sans Merci: A Ballad" in <u>The Norton Anthology of English Literature</u>. Ed. M.H. Abrams. New York: Norton, 1979.

King, Stephen. "Before the Play." <u>Whispers</u> 17/18 (August 1982): 19-47.

_____. <u>Carrie</u>. New York: New American Library, 1975.

_____. <u>Christine</u>. New York: New American Library, 1984.

_____. <u>Cujo</u>. New York: New American Library, 1982.

_____. <u>Danse Macabre</u>. New York: Berkley, 1982.

_____. <u>Firestarter</u>. New York: New American Library, 1981.

_____. "Imagery and the Third Eye." <u>The Writer</u> 93 (October 1980): 11-44.

_____. It. New York: Viking, 1986.

_____. Misery. New York: Viking, 1987.

_____. Pet Sematary. New York: Doubleday, 1983.

_____. Roadwork in The Bachman Books: Four Early Novels. New York: New American Library, 1985.

_____. 'Salem's Lot. New York: New American Library, 1976.

_____. "Strawberry Spring" in Night Shift. New York: New American Library, 1979.

_____. The Body in Different Seasons. New York: Viking, 1982.

_____. "The Boogeyman" in Night Shift. New York: New American Library, 1979.

_____. The Breathing Method in Different Seasons. New York: New American Library, 1983.

_____. The Dead Zone. New York: New American Library, 1980.

_____. The Mist in Skeleton Crew. New York: New American Library, 1986.

_____. "The Reach" in Skeleton Crew. New York: New American Library, 1986.

_____. The Shining. New York: New American Library, 1978.

_____. The Stand. New York: New American Library, 1979.

_____ (with Peter Straub). The Talisman. New York: Viking, 1984.

_____. Thinner. New York: New American Library, 1984.

_____. "Trucks" in <u>Night Shift</u>. New York: New American Library, 1979.

Martin, Terence. "The Method of Hawthorne's Tales" in <u>Nathaniel Hawthorne: A Collection of Criticism</u>. Ed. J. Donald Crowley. New York: McGraw-Hill, 1975.

McCammon, Robert R. Interview with Stanley Waiter. <u>Fantasy Review</u> 10 (May 1987): 22-24.

Melville, Herman. <u>Moby-Dick; or, the White Whale</u>. New York: Penguin, 1972.

Notkin, Deborah. "Stephen King: Horror and Humanity for Our Time" in <u>Fear Itself</u>. Eds. Tim Underwood and Chuck Miller. New York: New American Library, 1985.

O'Connor, Flannery. "The Fiction Writer and His Country" in <u>Mystery and Manners</u>. New York: Farrar, Straus, and Giroux, 1969.

Shelley, Mary. <u>Frankenstein</u>. London: Oxford University Press, 1969.

Skipp, John and Craig Spector. <u>The Cleanup</u>. New York: New American Library, 1987.

Steinbeck, John. <u>Of Mice and Men</u>. New York: Goodman, 1984.

Underwood, Tim. "The Skull Beneath the Skin" in <u>Kingdom of Fear</u>. Eds. Tim Underwood and Chuck Miller. New York: New American Library, 1986.

Winter, Douglas, ed. <u>Faces of Fear</u>. New York: Berkley Books, 1985.

_____. <u>The Art of Darkness: The Fiction of Stephen King</u>. New York: New American Library, 1984.

Zimmer, Heinrich. <u>The King and the Corpse</u>. New Jersey: Princeton University Press, 1957.

SELECTED BIBLIOGRAPHY

1. Primary Texts

    Novels

Carrie. Garden City, NY: Doubleday, 1974.
    NY: NAL, 1975.

Christine. West Kingston, RI: Donald M. Grant, 1983.
    NY: Viking, 1983.
    NY: NAL, 1984.

Cujo. NY: The Mysterious Press, 1981.
    NY: Viking, 1981.
    NY: NAL, 1982.

Cycle of the Werewolf. Westland, MI: Land of
    Enchantment, 1983.
    NY: NAL, 1984.

The Dead Zone. NY: Viking, 1979
    NY: NAL, 1980.

Firestarter. Huntington Woods, MI: Phantasia
    Press, 1980.
    NY: Viking, 1980.
    NY: NAL, 1981.

It. NY: Viking, 1986.
    NY: NAL, 1987.

The Long Walk. As Richard Bachman. NY: NAL, 1979.

Misery. NY: Viking, 1987.

Pet Sematary. Garden City, NY: Doubleday, 1983.
    NY: NAL, 1984.

Rage. As Richard Bachman. NY: NAL, 1982.

Roadwork. As Richard Bachman. NY: NAL, 1981.

The Running Man. As Richard Bachman. NY: NAL, 1982.

'Salem's Lot. Garden City, NY: Doubleday, 1977.
    NY: NAL, 1978.

The Stand. Garden City, NY: Doubleday, 1978.

The Talisman. With Peter Straub. West Kingston,
    RI: Donald M. Grant, 1984.
    NY: Viking and Putnam, 1984.
    NY: Berkley, 1985.

Thinner. As Richard Bachman. NY: NAL, 1984.

    Collections

The Bachman Books: Four Early Novels. NY: NAL,
    1985.

Creepshow. NY: NAL, 1982.

The Dark Tower. West Kingston, RI: Donald M.
    Grant, 1982.

Different Seasons. NY: Viking, 1982.
    NY: NAL, 1983.

Night Shift. Garden City, NY: Doubleday, 1978.
    NY: NAL, 1983.

Skeleton Crew. NY: Putnam, 1985
    NY: NAL, 1986.

Stephen King. NY: William Heinemann, Inc. and
    Octopus Books, 1981.

Nonfiction

Danse Macabre. NY: Everest House, 1981.
    NY: Berkley, 1982.

2.   Full-Length Studies of King's Works

Browne, Ray and Gary Hoppenstand, eds. The Gothic
    World of Stephen King: Landscape of
    Nightmares. Bowling Green, OH: Bowling Green
    State University Popular Press, 1987.
    Collection of critical essays on King's life
    and fiction.

Collings, Michael R. *The Films of Stephen King*. Mercer Island, WA: Starmont House, (in progress).

----------. *The Many Facets of Stephen King*. Mercer Island, WA: Starmont House, 1985.

----------. *Stephen King as Richard Bachman*. Mercer Island, WA: Starmont House, 1985.

----------. *The Stephen King Concordance*. Mercer Island, WA: Starmont House, 1985.

----------. *The Stephen King Phenomenon*. Mercer Island, WA: Starmont House, 1986.

Collings, Michael R. and David A. Engebretson. *The Shorter Works of Stephen King*. Mercer Island, WA: Starmont House, 1985.

Horsting, Jessie. *Stephen King at the Movies*. New York: Starlog Press, 1986.

Magistrale, Tony. *Landscape of Fear: Stephen King's American Gothic*. Bowling Green, OH: Bowling Green State University Popular Press, 1987.

----------, ed. *The Shining Reader*. Mercer Island, WA: Starmont House, (in progress).

Schweitzer, Darrell, ed. *Discovering Stephen King*. Mercer Island, WA: Starmont House, 1985.

Underwood, Tim and Chuck Miller, eds. *Fear Itself: The Horror Fiction of Stephen King*. San Francisco, CA: Underwood-Miller, 1982 [limited, hardcover]; New York: NAL/Plume, 1984 [paper-back].

----------. *Kingdom of Fear: The World of Stephen King*. New York: NAL, 1986.

Van Hise, James. *Enterprise Incidents Presents Stephen King*. Tampa, FL: New Media, 1984.

Winter, Douglas E. <u>The Reader's Guide to Stephen King</u>. Mercer Island, WA: Starmont House, 1985.

----------. <u>Stephen King: The Art of Darkness</u>. NY: NAL, 1984.

Zagorski, Edward J. <u>Teacher's Manual: The Novels of Stephen King</u>. New York: NAL, 1981 [pamphlet].

3. Selected Critical Articles and Reviews

Adams, Michael. "<u>Danse Macabre</u>." In <u>Magill's Literary Annual 1982</u>, Vol. I. Ed. Frank N. Magill. Englewood Cliffs, NJ: Salem Press, 1982.

Albertson, Jim and Peter S. Perakos. "<u>The Shining</u>." <u>Cinefantastique</u> 7 (1978).

Alexander, Alex E. "Stephen King's <u>Carrie</u>--A Universal Fairy Tale." <u>Journal of Popular Culture</u> (Fall 1969).

Allen, Mel. "The Man Who Writes Nightmares." <u>Yankee Magazine</u> (March 1979).

Alpert, Michael. "Designing <u>The Eyes of the Dragon</u>." <u>Castle Rock</u> (August 1985).

Ashley, Mike. "Stephen King." In <u>Who's Who in Horror and Fantasy Fiction</u>. New York: Taplinger, 1977.

Atchity, Kenneth. "Stephen King: Making Burgers With the Best." <u>Los Angeles Times Book Review</u> 20 August 1982.

"Bachman Revealed to be Stephen King Alias." <u>Publishers Weekly</u> 22 March 1985.

Bagnato, Teresa. "'Shining' at the Overlook Hotel." <u>Castle Rock</u> (February-March, May 1985).

Bandler, Michael J. "The Horror Is as Much Political as Biological." *Newsday* 19 October 1980.

──────────. "The King of the Macabre at Home." *Parents* (January 1982).

Barkham, John. "A Story Fired with Imagination, Protest." *Philadelphia Inquirer* 31 August 1980.

Barron, Neil. "'Bachman' Indeed Reads Like Stephen King." *Fantasy Review* (March 1985). Review of *Thinner*.

Barry, Dave. "*Christine* Is Demon for Punishment." *Philadelphia Inquirer* 27 March 1983.

Beahm, George. "Collecting Stephen King Limiteds." *Castle Rock* (May 1985).

Bentkowski, Kent Daniel. "A Skeleton Crew Inside King's Closet." *Castle Rock* (August 1985).

Bishop, Michael. "Mad Dogs . . . and Englishmen." *Washington Post Book World* 23 August 1981; as "The Saint Bernard That Becomes an Engine of Madness and Death." *San Francisco Chronicle Review* 20 September 1981.

Blakemore, Bill. "Kubrick's 'Shining' Secret." *The Washington Post* 12 July 1987.

Bleiler, Richard. "Stephen King." In *Supernatural Writers: Fantasy and Horror*. Ed. E.F. Bleiler. New York: Scribners, 1985.

Boonstra, John. "King of the Creeps." *Hartford Advocate* 27 October 1982.

Boyer, P. Book Review of Clecak's *America's Quest for the Ideal Self*. *Journal of American History* 70 (1984). References to King's fiction.

Bradley, Marion Zimmer. "Fandom: Its Value to the Professional." In *Inside Outer Space*. Ed. Sharton Jarvis. New York: Ungar, 1985. References to King and fandom.

Briggs, Joe Bob. "Big Steve is the Cat's Pajamas." *USA Today* 8 May 1985. Review of *Cat's Eye*.

Bromell, Henry. "The Dimming of Stanley Kubrick." *Atlantic*. (August 1980).

Brown, Stephen. "The Real Beginning of the Real Bachman." *Castle Rock* (May 1985).

----------. "Stephen King, Shining Through." *Washington Post* 9 April 1985.

----------. "The Works of Richard Bachman." *Washington Post* 9 April 1984.

Bryant, Edward. "The Future in Words." *Mile High Futures* (May 1983; January 1984). Review of *Pet Sematary*.

Budrys, Algis. "Books." *The Magazine of Fantasy and Science Fiction* (February 1983).

----------. "A Doggy New Novel from Stephen King." *Chicago Sun-Times* 6 September 1981.

----------. "King's *Firestarter*: It's Hot Stuff, All Right." *Chicago Sun-Times* 21 September 1980.

----------. "Stephen King's Car: Repossessed by the Devil." *Chicago Sun-Times Book Week* 3 May 1981.

----------. "The Wolf-Mask of Horror, As Lifted by Stephen King." *Chicago Sun-Times Book Week* 3 May 1981.

Callendar, Newgate. "Criminals at Large." *New York Times Book Review* 26 May 1974.

Cannon, Leslie. "Where the Conscious Meets the Subconscious." *Cincinnati Enquirer* 6 April 1978.

Carmichael, Carrie. "Who's Afraid of Stephen (Carrie) King?" *Family Weekly* 6 January 1980.

Carter, Erskine. "King is Dead. Long Live the Kings." *Castle Rock* (September 1985).

Casey, Susan. "On the Set of *'Salem's Lot*." *Fangoria* (February 1980).

"*Cat's Eye* Reviews." *Castle Rock* (June 1985).

Chandler, Randy. "Horror Master Tells Motor-Vating Tale." *Atlanta Journal-Constitution* 17 April 1983.

"Checking In: Stephen King." *Boston Magazine* (October 1980).

Cheever, Leonard. "Apocalypse and the Popular Imagination: Stephen King's *The Stand*." *Artes Liberales* 8 (Fall 1981).

Cheuse, Alan. "Horror Writer's Holiday." *New York Times Book Review* 29 August 1982.

Childs, Mike and Alan Jones. "De Palma Has the Power." *Cinefantastique* (Summer 1977).

Chow, Dan. "*Locus* Looks at More Books." *Locus* (April 1983).

Christensen, Dan. "Stephen King: Living in Constant Deadly Terror." *Bloody Best of Fangoria* (1982).

Chute, David. "King Gives Second-Best Horror Effort in *Cujo*." *Los Angeles Herald Examiner* 9 September 1981.

----------. "Reign of Horror." *Boston Phoenix* 9 December 1980.

Clayton, Bill and Debra Clayton. "Stephen King: The King of the Beasties." Chillers. (November 1981).

Cline, Edward. "Dark Doings in King Country." Wall Street Journal 28 October 1983.

Collings, Michael R. "Collings Studies Stephen King." Castle Rock: The Stephen King Newsletter (June 1985). Excerpt from Stephen King as Richard Bachman.

----------. Review of Skeleton Crew. Fantasy Review (June 1985).

Collins, Robert A. "Weinberg Gets Last Laugh." Fantasy Review (March 1985).

Collins, Tom. "Frank Belknap Long on Literature, Lovecraft, and the Golden Age of Weird Tales." Twilight Zone Magazine (January 1982). Assessment of King as modern writer.

Cortland, Will. "The King of Bumps in the Night." Dodge Adventurer (Spring 1985); Castle Rock (June 1985).

Counts, Kyle. Review of Children of the Corn (film). Cinefantastique (September 1984).

----------. Review of Cujo (film). Cinefantastique (December/January 1983/1984).

Cruz, Manny. "Search for Terror is Worth King's Ransom." Castle Rock (September 1985).

Davis, Joanne. "Trade News: Bachman Revealed to Be Stephen King Alias." Publishers Weekly 22 March 1985.

Davis, L. J. "A Shabby Dog Story from Stephen King." Chicago Tribune Book World 16 August 1981.

De Lint, Charles. Review of The Eyes of the Dragon. Fantasy Review. (July 1985).

Demarest, Michael. "Hot Moppet." *Time* 15 September 1980.

Dimeo, Steve. "Firestarter." *Cinefantastique* (January 1985).

Disch, Thomas. "Books." *Twilight Zone* (April 1984).

Dudley, Alberta. "My First Science Fiction Convention." *Castle Rock* (September 1985). King books on sale at convention.

Edwards, Phil. "*The Shining*." *Starburst* (1980).

Edwards, Thomas R. Review of *It*. *New York Review of Books* 18 December 1986.

Egan, James. "Antidetection: Gothic and Detective Conventions in the Fiction of Stephen King." *Clues* 5 (Spring/Summer 1984).

----------. "Apocalypticism in the Fiction of Stephen King." *Extrapolation* (Fall 1984).

----------. "A Single Powerful Spectacle: Stephen King's Gothic Melodrama." *Extrapolation* (Spring 1986).

Ehlers, Leigh A. "*Carrie*: Book and Film." *Literature Film Quarterly* (Spring 1981). Rpt. *Ideas of Order in Literature and Film*. Ed. Peter Ruppert. Talahassie, FL: University of Florida Press, 1980.

Ellis, Ray and Katalin Ellis. "The Night of the Horror King." *Cinefantastique* (May 1985).

Eng, Steve. "Fantasy Writers Focus of Study." *The Tennessean Sunday Bookcase* 23 January 1983. Review of *Fear Itself* and Winter's *The Reader's Guide to Stephen King*.

Everett, David. "Stephen King's *Children of the Corn*." *Fangoria*, 35 (April 1984).

----------. "Stephen King's *Silver Bullet*." *Fangoria*, 48 (1985).

----------. "Of Roaches and Snakes." Fangoria, 20 (May 1982). Discussion of Ray Mendes' work on Creepshow.

Fantasy Mongers 13 (Winter 1984/1985). Review of Winter's The Art of Darkness.

----------. 13 (Winter 1984/1985). Review of Thinner.

"Fantasy Review Article is a Hoax!" Castle Rock (June 1985).

Ferguson, Mary. "'Strawberry Spring': Stephen King's Gothic Universe." Footsteps V (April 1985).

Fiedler, Leslie. "Fantasy as Commodity, Pornography, Camp and Myth." Presented to the International Conference on the Fantastic in the Arts, March 1984; Fantasy Review (June 1984).

Fleischer, Leonore. "Big Bucks." Publishers Weekly 6 September 1985.

Foltz, Kim and Penelope Wang. "An Unstoppable Thriller King." Newsweek 10 June 1985.

Frane, Jeff. "Locus Looks at More Books." Locus (August 1982).

----------. "A Stunning Storyteller." Seattle Times Magazine 4 February 1979.

Frank, Janrae. "Stephen King's Night Shift: Student Shorts of Stephen King Tales Headed for Videocassette Release." Cinefantastique (July 1985).

French, Lawrence. "Cat's Eye." Cinefantastique (October 1985).

Gagne, Paul. "Catching up with the Rapidly Rising Star of Author Stephen King: Thoughts on Books, Films, and What Went Wrong on The Shining." Cinefantastique 10 (1980).

----------. "<u>Creepshow</u>: Five Jolting Tales of
   Horror! from Stephen King and George Romero."
   <u>Cinefantastique</u> (April 1982).

----------. "<u>Creepshow</u>: It's an $8 Million Comic
   Book, from George Romero and Friends."
   <u>Cinefantastique</u> (September/October 1982).

----------. "<u>Creepshow</u>: Masters of the Macabre."
   <u>Cinefantastique</u> (September/October 1982).

----------. "<u>Salem's Lot</u>." <u>Famous Monsters of
   Filmland</u> (April 1980).

----------. "Stephen King." <u>Cinefantastique</u> 10
   (1980).

----------. "Stephen King." <u>Cinefantastique</u>
   (December/January 1983-84).

----------. "Stephen King: The Master of the
   Horror Novel Abandons Television and Turns to
   Writing for the Screen." <u>Cinefantastique</u> 10
   (1980).

Garcia, Guy D. "People." <u>Time</u> 9 September 1985.
   Comments on <u>Maximum Overdrive</u>.

Gareffa, Peter M. "Stephen King." <u>Contemporary
   Authors</u>, New Revision Series, I.

Geduld, Harry M. "Mazes and Murders." <u>The Humanist</u>
   (September/October 1980).

Geoghegan, Bill and Tom Simon. Editorials and
   columns in <u>King's Crypt</u>. From July 1985.

Gifford, Thomas, "Stephen King's Quartet."
   <u>Washington Post Book World</u>. 22 August 1982.

Goldberg, Lee. "Now Re-Entering 'The Twilight
   Zone.'" <u>Starlog</u>, 99 (October 1985).
   References to King.

Goldstein, Toby. "Stephen King's Scary Monsters
   Live Right Next Door." <u>Creem</u> (October 1982).

Goodwin, Michael. "The 'Film Script as Novel' Scam." Boulevards (January 1981).

Gorner, Peter. "King Drives at Horror with Less-Than-Usual Fury." Chicago Tribune 6 April 1983.

Goshagarian, Gary. "Goshagarian Finds the Real Stephen King." Castle Rock (August 1985). Address presented to the Hartford College of Women, 24 April 1985.

Graham, Mark. "Critics Dissect Horror of Stephen King's Work." Rocky Mountain News. Review of Fear Itself.

----------. "A Dance into Horror with Stephen King." Rocky Mountain News.

----------. "Dark Forces: Anthology of Horror." Rocky Mountain News 5 October 1980.

----------. "Dark Tower Shows King in Different Light." Rocky Mountain News 1 August 1982.

----------. "Good News for Horror Buffs." Rocky Mountain News 11 May 1984. Review of Shadowings.

----------. "Macabre Master." Rocky Mountain News 4 December 1983. Review of Pet Sematary and Cycle of the Werewolf.

----------. "Masters of the Macabre." Rocky Mountain News 7 October 1984. Review of The Talisman.

----------. "Moral Dilemma in Latest Novel by Stephen King." Rocky Mountain News 9 September 1979. Review of The Dead Zone.

----------. "Mouth Foaming for Good Scare?" Rocky Mountain News 6 September 1981.

----------. "New King Novel Will Frighten You." Rocky Mountain News 14 September 1980. Review of Firestarter.

----------. "Revealing Work Examines King-Bachman Connection." *Rocky Mountain News* 15 September 1985. Review of *Stephen King as Richard Bachman*.

----------. "Stephen King Causes a 'Fury' of a Monster, 1958 Vintage." *Rocky Mountain News* 8 May 1983.

----------. "Stephen King Shows Another Grisly Side." *Rocky Mountain News* 19 September 1982. Review of *Different Seasons*.

----------. "Stephen King Stories Never Seem to Die." *Rocky Mountain News* 16 June 1985. Review of *Skeleton Crew*.

Granger, Bill. "Stephen King Stikes Again." *Chicago Tribune Book World* 24 August 1980.

Grant, Charles L., David Morrell, Alan Ryan, and Douglas E. Winter. "Different Writers on *Different Seasons*." *Fantasy Newsletter* (February 1983); in *Shadowings*. Ed. Douglas E. Winter. Mercer Island, WA: Starmont House, 1983.

Grant, Donald M. "Stephen King as Breckinridge Elkins?" *Castle Rock* (May 1985).

Gray, Paul. "Master of Postliterate Prose." *Time* 20 August 1982.

Grobaty, Time. "Stephen King Thinks It's Fun to 'Get the Reader.'" *Watertown Daily Times* 18 September 1980.

Hall, Melissa Mia. "A Bestseller that Foams at the Mouth." *Fort Worth Star-Telegram* 23 August 1981.

Hansen, Ron. "*Creepshow*: The Dawn of a Living Horror Comedy." *Esquire* (January 1981).

Hard, Annette. "King: Novellas from a Consummate Story Teller." *Houston Chronicle* 12 September 1982.

Harper, L. Christine. "Christine" (Reel Futures). Mile High Futures 22 January 1984.

Harris, Judith. P. "Timid, One-Note Stories need Padding to Fill Even 30 Minutes." Cinefantastique (July 1985). Review of Tales from the Darkside ("The Word Processor").

----------. "King: Sailing Uncharted Seas." Houston Chronicle 7 October 1979.

Hatlen, Burton. "Alumnmus Publishes Symbolic Novel, Shows Promise." The Maine Campus 12 April 1974.

----------. "The Destruction and Re-Creation of the Human Community in Stephen King's The Stand." Presented to the International Conference on the Fantastic in the Arts, March 1984; Footsteps V (April 1982).

----------. "The Mad Dog and Maine." In Shadowings. Ed. Douglas E. Winter. Mercer Island, WA: Starmont House, 1983.

----------. "'Salem's Lot Critiques American Civilization." The Maine Campus 12 December 1975.

----------. "Steve King's The Stand." Kennebec (April 1979).

----------. "Steve King's Third Novel Shines On" The Maine Campus 1 April 1977.

Herndon, Ben. "Real Tube Terror." Twilight Zone Magazine (December 1985).

Hewitt, Tim. "Cat's Eye." Cinefantastique (May 1985).

----------. "Cat's Eye." Cinefantastique (October 1985).

----------. "Silver Bullet." Cinefantastique (May 1985).

Hitchens, C. "American Notes." The Times Literary Suppliment 4219 (1984).

Hofsess, John. "Kubrick: Critics Be Damned." Soho News (NY) 28 May 1980.

Hogan, David J. "The Dead Zone." Cinefantastique (December/January 1983/1984).

----------. "Firestarter." Cinefantastique (September 1984).

Horsting, Jessica. "Cat's Eye." Fantastic Films (June 1985).

----------. "Cujo: The Movie." Fantastic Films (November 1983).

Indick, Ben P. "Stephen King As an Epic Writer." In Discovering Modern Horror Fiction, I. Ed. Darrell Schweitzer. Mercer Island, WA: Starmont House, 1985.

Jameson, Richard T. "Kubrick's Shining." Film Comment (July/August 1980).

Johnson, Kim. "Christine: Stephen King and John Carpenter Take a Joy Ride into Terror!" Mediascene Prevue (1983).

Kauffman, Stanley. "The Dulling." New Republic 14 June 1980.

Kaveney, Roz. "The Consolations of Terror." Books & Bookmen (November 1981).

Keeler, Greg. "The Shining: Ted Kramer Has a Nightmare." Journal of Popular Film and Television (Winter 1981).

Kelley, Bill. "Cat's Eye." Cinefantastique (July 1985).

----------. "John Carpenter's Christine: Bringing Stephen King's Best Seller to the Screen." Cinefantastique (September 1983).

----------. "King's *Firestarter* Stretches Boundaries of Macabre Fiction." *Fort Lauderdale News/Sun Sentinel* 28 September 1980.

----------. "*Salem's Lot*: Filming Horror for Television." *Cinefantastique* (Winter 1979).

Kendrick, Walter. "Stephen King Gets Eminent." *Village Voice* 29 April/5 May 1981.

Kennedy, Harlan. "Kubrick Goes Gothic." *American Film* (June 1980).

Kilbourne, Dan. "*Christine*." In *Magill's Cinema Annual 1984*. Ed. Frank N. Magill. Englewood Cliffs, NY: Salem Press, 1984.

Kimberling, Ronald C. *Kenneth Burke's Dramatism and Popular Arts*. Bowling Green, OH: Bowling Green State University Popular Press, 1982.

King, Tabitha. "Living with the Bogey Man." In *Murderess, Ink.* Ed. Dilys Winn. New York: Bell, 1979.

"King's Too Fast for His Own Good." *Los Angeles Daily News* 11 April 1985.

Klavan, Andrew. "The Pleasure of the Subtext: Stephen King's Id-Life Crisis." *Village Voice* 3 March 1987.

Klein, Jeanne. "King Recycles a Chilling Tale." *Seattle Post-Intelligencer* 6 May 1985.

Kroll, Jack. "Stanley Kubrick's Horror Show." *Newsweek* 26 May 1980.

Lawson, Carol. "Stephen King." *The New York Times Book Review* 23 September 1979.

Leerhsen, Charles. "The Titans of Terror." *Newsweek* 24 December 1984. King and Straub.

Lehmann-Haupt, Christopher. "Books of the Times."
New York Seattle Post-Intelligencer 26 August
1979.

----------. "Books of the Times." New York Times
8 September 1980; as "This Girl May Set World
Afire." Omaha World-Herald 14 September 1980;
as "A Little Girl's Pyrotechnics." Seattle
Post-Intelligencer 21 September 1980.

----------. "Books of the Times." New York Times
14 April 1981; as "Danse Macabre to Appeal to
Lovers of Grisly Stories." Omaha World-Herald
26 April 1981.

----------. "Books of the Times." New York Times
14 August 1981.

----------. "Books of the Times." New York Times
11 August 1982.

----------. "Books of the Times." New York Times
12 April 1983.

----------. "Books of the Times." New York Times
21 October 1983; as "Finally, a Story to Scare
Stephen King." Denver Post 30 October 1983.

Leiber, Fritz. "Fantasy Books." Locus (April
1980). Review of The Dead Zone.

----------. "On Fantasy." Fantasy Newsletter 39
(August 1981).

----------. "Whispering in the Shadows."
Washington Post Book World 12 April 1981.

Leonard, Stephanie. Editorials and Columns in
Castle Rock: The Stephen King Newsletter.
From January 1985.

----------. "Stephen King Bibliography: Parts I
and II." Castle Rock (June/July 1985).

Levin, Martin. "Genre Items." New York Times
Book Review 4 February 1979.

Lidston, Robert. "<u>Dracula</u> and <u>Salem's Lot</u>: Why the Monsters Won't Die." <u>West Virginia University Philological Papers</u> 28 (1982).

Lingeman, Richard R. "Something Nasty in the Tub." <u>New York Times</u> 1 March 1977.

Lorenz, Janet. "<u>Carrie</u>." In <u>Magill's Survey of Cinema</u>. Vol. I. Ed. Frank N. Magill. Englewood Cliffs, NJ: Salem Press, 1981.

Lucas, Time. "David Cronenberg's <u>The Dead Zone</u>." <u>Cinefantastique</u> 14 (December/January 1983/1984).

Luciano, Dale. "<u>Danse Macabre</u>: Stephen King Surveys the Field of Horror." <u>The Comics Journal</u> 72 (May 1982).

----------. "E. C. Horror Stories Mistranslated into Film." <u>The Comics Journal</u> 79 (January 1983).

Lyons, Gene. "King of High-School Horror." <u>Newsweek</u> 2 May 1983.

McDonnell, David. "The Once and Future King." <u>Prevue</u> (May 1982).

McDonnell, David and John Sayers. "<u>Creepshow</u>." <u>Mediascene Prevue</u> (May 1982).

McDowell, Edwin. "Behind the Bestsellers." <u>New York Times Book Review</u> 27 September 1981.

McLellan, Joseph. "Vision of Holocaust." <u>Washington Post</u> 30 August 1979.

Macklin, F. Anthony. "Understanding Kubrick: <u>The Shining</u>." <u>Journal of Popular Television and Film</u> (Summer 1981).

Magill, Frank N., ed. <u>Survey of Modern Fantasy Literature</u>. Englewood Cliffs, NJ: Salem Press, 1983.

Magistrale, Anthony S. "'Barriers Not Meant to be Broken': Where the Horror Springs in Stephen King." Combustable Goods: Proceedings of the Northeast Popular Culture Association. Orono, Maine: University of Maine Press, 1988.

----------. "Crumbling Castles of Sand: The Social Landscape of Stephen King's Gothic Vision." Journal of Popular Literature 1 (Fall/Winter 1985).

----------. "Hawthorne's Woods Revisited: Stephen King's Pet Sematary." Nathaniel Hawthorne Review (Spring 1988).

----------. "Inherited Haunts: Stephen King's Terrible Children." Extrapolation 27 (Spring 1985).

----------. "Stephen King's Vietnam Allegory: an Interpretation of 'Children of the Corn.'" Presented to the International Conference on the Fantastic in the Arts, March 1984; Cuyahoga Review (Spring/Summer 1984); Footsteps V (April 1985).

Malpezzi, Frances M. and William M. Clements. "The Shining." In Magill's Survey of Cinema. Vol. V. Ed. Frank N. Magill. Englewood Cliffs, NJ: Salem Press, 1981.

Martin, Robert. "A Casual Chat with Mr. George A. Romero." Fangoria (October 1982).

----------. "Creepshow." Twilight Zone Magazine (September 1982).

----------. "Interview with a Werewolf." Fangoria 44 (1985).

----------. "Keith Gordon and Christine." Fangoria 32 (1983).

----------. "Mark Lester Directs Firestarter." Fangoria, 36 (1984).

----------. "On (and Off) the Set of Creepshow."
    Fangoria (July 1982).

----------. "On the Set of Firestarter."
    Fangoria 35 (1984).

----------. "Richard Kobritz and Christine."
    Fangoria 32 (1983).

----------. "Stephen King's Silver Bullet."
    Fangoria 48 (1985).

Mayer, Sheryl. "An Evening with Stephen King at
    Amherst." Castle Rock (May 1985).

Mayersburg, Paul. "Overlook Hotel." Sight and
    Sound (Winter 1980-1981).

Meyer, Richard E. "Stephen King." In Beacham's
    Popular Fiction in America. Vol 2. Ed. Walton
    Beacham. Washington: Beacham Publishing
    Company, 1986. Overview of King's life,
    career, and literary reception.

Mewshaw, Michael. "Novels and Stories." New York
    Times Book Review 26 March 1978.

"Mild Down-Easter Discovers Terror Is the Ticket."
    People 29 December 1980 - 5 January 1981.

Moore, Darrell. The Best, Worst, and Most Unusual
    Horror Films. Skokie, IL: Publications
    International, 1983 (hardcover).
    Discussions of Carrie and The Shining.

Moritz, Charles. "Stephen King." Contemporary
    Biography Yearbook 1981. New York: H. H.
    Wilson, 1981.

Morrison, Michael A. "Pet Sematary: Opposing
    Views...Finest Horror Ever Written." Fantasy
    Review 64 (January 1984).

Munster, Bill. "An Interview with Douglas E.
    Winter." Footsteps V (April 1985).

Naha, Ed. "Front Row Seats at the Creepshow."
    Twilight Zone Magazine (May 1982).

Nathan, Paul S. "Helping Hand." Publishers
Weekly 30 August 1985.

----------. "The Talisman and the Clubs."
"Publishers Weekly 23 November 1984.

Neilson, Keith. "The Dead Zone." In Magill's
Literary Annual 1980, Vol I. Ed. Frank N.
Magill. Englewood Cliffs, NJ: Salem Press,
1980 (hardcover).

----------. "Different Seasons." In Magill's
Literary Annual 1983, Vol. I. Ed. Frank N.
Magill. Englewood Cliffs, NJ: Salem Press,
1980.

----------. "King Gets Compatible Critic."
Fantasy Review (March 1985). Review of
Winter's Stephen King: The Art of Darkness.

Nelson, Thomas A. Kubrick: Inside the Artist's
Maze. Bloomington, IN: Indiana University
Press, 1982. Chapter on The Shining.

Neuhaus, Cable. "Firestarter's Premier Was A
Critical Fizzle..." People 28 May 1984.

Norulak, Frank. "Searching for Richard Bachman."
Castle Rock (September 1985).

Novak, Ralph. "Firestarter." People 28 May 1984.

Osbourne, Linda B. "The Supernatural Con Man vs.
the Hymn-Singing Mother." Washington Post 23
November 1978.

Patrouch, Jr., Joseph F. "Stephen King in
Context." In Patterns of the Fantastic. Ed.
Donald M. Hassler. Mercer Island, WA:
Starmont House, 1983.

Pautz, Peter J. Review of Christine. Science
Fiction & Fantasy Book Review (SFRA) 16 (July-
August 1983).

Pearce, Howard D. "The Shining as Lichtung: Kubrick's Film, Heidegger's Clearing." In Forms of the Fantastic: Selected Essays from the Third International Conference on the Fantastic in Literature and Film. New York: Greenwood, 1986.

Pettus, David, ed. Fan Plus. 1984. Stephen King issue.

Phippen, Sanford. "Stephen King's Appeal to Youth." Maine Life (December 1980).

Podhoretz, John. "The Magnificent Revels of Stephen King." Wall Street Journal 4 September 1980.

Proch, Paul and Charles Kaufman. "Eggboiler." National Lampoon (May 1984). Parody of Firestarter.

Radburn, Barry. "Stephen King and John Carpenter: Cruisin' with Christine." Footsteps V (April 1985).

Rebeaux, Max. "Twilight Zone." Cinefantastique 15 (October 1985).

Reuter, Madalynne. "502,000 Copies of Talisman Shipped in One Day." Publishers Weekly 26 October 1984.

Riggenbach, Jeff. "Suspense Accelerates in King's Christine." San Jose Mercury News 1 May 1983.

Rolfe, John. "Fitting Author Stephen King to the Charles Dickens Mold." Maine Sunday Telegram 19 September 1982.

Roraback, Dick. "Gift of Sight: Visions from a Nether World." Los Angeles Times Book Review 26 August 1979.

Rosenbaum, Mary Helene. "Pet Sematary." Christian Century 21 March 1984.

Rudin, S. "The Urban Gothic, From Translyvania to
    the South Bronx." *Extrapolation* 25 (1984).
    Discussion of *Christine* and *Danse Macabre*.

Ryan, Alan. "Ride into Horror with *Christine*."
    Cleveland Plain Dealer 17 April 1983.

Ryan, Desmond. "The Scariest Movie Ever Made."
    Saga (July 1980).

----------. "Stephen King Departs from Horror."
    Cleveland Plain Dealer 26 September 1982.

Salamon, Julie. "Horrormonger Stephen King on
    Screen." *Wall Street Journal* 25 April 1985.
    Review of *Cat's Eye*.

Sallee, Wayne Allen. "No Bones About It." *Castle
    Rock* (August 1985). Review of *Skeleton Crew*.

----------. "*Thinner*: A Thinly Disguised King
    Novel." *Castle Rock* (May 1985).

Sanders, Joe. Review of *The Talisman*. *Fantasy
    Review* (February 1985).

Scapperotti, Dan. "Tales from the Darkside."
    Cinefantastique (January 1985).

Schaefer, S. "The Director is King." *Film Comment*
    22 (1986).

Schiff, Stuart David. "The Glorious Past, Erratic
    Present, and Questionable Future of the
    Specialty Presses." In *Inside Outer Space*.
    Ed. Sharon Jarvis. New York: Ungar, 1985.

Schneider, Peter. "Collecting the Works of
    Stephen King." *AB Bookman's Weekly* 24 October
    1983.

Schow, David J. "Return of the Curse of the Son
    of Mr. King: Book Two." *Whispers*, No. 17/18
    (August 1982).

Schweitzer, Darrell. "Introduction." In
   Discovering Modern Horror Fiction,I. Ed.
   Darrell Schweitzer. Mercer Island WA:
   Starmont House, 1985. King's influence on
   horror fiction.

Science Fiction Book Club brochure. "Stephen
   King." (August 1985).

Scott, Pete. "The Shadow Exploded." Dark
   Horizons (Summer 1982).

See, Carolyn. "A Bumper Crop of Killing." Los
   Angeles Times 8 May 1983.

Seelye, John. "Wizard of Ooze with Four Novellas
   Makes Poe a Piker." Chicago Tribune Bookworld
   22 August 1982.

Sherman, David. "Nightmare Library." Fangoria
   (April 1984). Review of Cycle.

Shiner, Lewis. "A Collision of Good and Evil."
   Dallas Morning News 26 November 1978.

Shreffler, Philip A. "For Chills and Thrills."
   St. Louis Post-Dispatch 5 October 1980.

Simon, John. "Horrible Vision." National Review 27
   June 1980.

Slung, Michelle. "A Master of the Macabre." The
   New Republic 21 February 1981; expanded as "In
   the Matter of Stephen King." Armchair
   Detective (Spring 1981); rpt. Castle Rock
   (September 1985).

----------. "Scare Tactics." New York Times Book
   Review 10 May 1981.

Smith, Joan. "Pseudonym Kept Five King Novels a
   Mystery." Bangor Daily News 9 February 1985.

Squires, Roy A. "Science Fiction and Fantasy: An
   Overview." AB Bookman's Weekly 24 October
   1983. Reference to King.

Sragow, Michael. "Stephen King's <u>Creepshow</u>: The Aesthetics of Gross-out." <u>Rolling Stone</u> 25 November 1982.

Stamm, Michael E. Review of <u>Cycle of the Werewolf</u>. <u>Science Fiction & Fantasy Review</u> (March 1984).

----------. "<u>Pet Sematary</u>: Opposing Views...Flawed, Unsatisfying." <u>Fantasy Review</u> 64 (January 1984).

----------. Review of <u>Pet Sematary</u>. <u>Science Fiction & Fantasy Book Review</u> (SFRA) 20 (December 1983).

Stasio, Marilyn. "High Suspense." <u>Penthouse</u> (July 1983).

"Stephen King." <u>Contemporary Literary Criticism</u>, Vol. 12. Eds. Dedria Bryfonski and Garard Senick. Detroit, MI: Gale Research, 1980.

"Stephen King." <u>Current Biography Yearbook, 1981</u>. Ed. Charles Moritz. New York: H. W. Wilson, 1981.

"Stephen King Makes Millions by Scaring Hell Out of Three Million Readers." <u>People</u> 7 March 1981.

"Stephen King's Torrent of Horror." <u>USA Today</u> 11 July 1985.

Stewart, Robert. "The Rest of King." <u>Starship: The Magazine About Science Fiction</u>. 18 (Spring 1981).

"Straub Talks About <u>Talisman</u>." <u>Castle Rock</u> (July 1985).

Strouse, Jean. "Beware of the Dog." <u>Newsweek</u> 31 August 1981.

Sullivan, Jack. "Two Ways to Write a Gothic." <u>New York Times Book Review</u> 20 February 1977.

Suplee, Curt. "Stricken a la King." Washington Post 26 August 1980.

Thompson, Andrea. "The Thrills, Chills, and Skills of Stephen King." McCall's (February 1983).

Thompson, Thomas. "King's Latest a Shaggy Rabid Dog Story." Los Angeles Times 6 September 1981; as "Cujo: Tale About a Mad Dog Ought to be Put to Sleep." Baltimore News American 6 September 1981.

Todorov, Tzvetan. The Fantastic: A Structural Approach to a Literary Genre. Ithaca: Cornell University Press, 1975.

Tuchman, Michael. "From Niagara-on-the-Lake, Ontario." Film Comment 19 (May-June 1983). Interview with Cronenberg on The Dead Zone.

Van Rjndt, Phillipe. "The Other Woman Was a Car." New York Times Book Review 3 April 1983.

Vernier, James. "Christine" Twilight Zone Magazine (February 1984).

----------. "On the Set of Dead Zone." Twilight Zone Magazine (December 1983).

----------. "Zeroing in on the Dead Zone." Twilight Zone Magazine (November/December 1983).

Wager, Walter. Review of It. New York Times Book Review 24 August 1986.

Wells, Jeffrey. "Creepshow Crawlers Can Cause Creepy Cold Chills." New York Post 3 September 1981.

Westerbeck, Collin. "The Waning of Stanley Kubrick." Commonweal 1 August 1980.

Wiater, Stanley. "Danse Macabre." Valley Advocate 27 May 1981.

----------. "Dark Stars Rising." Valley Advocate 8 April 1981.

----------. "Just Your Average Guy." Valley Advocate 27 May 1981.

----------. "Stephen King and George Romero: Collaboration in Terror." Fangoria (June 1980).

Williams, Paul. "Fit for a King: Fascination with Horror Stories." Los Angeles Times 10 May 1981.

Williams, Sharon. "Stephen King's Cycle of the Werewolf Becomes Silver Bullet for the Silver Screen." Fantastic Films (October 1985).

Willis, John. "Christine." in Screen World 1983. New York: Crown, 1984.

----------. "Creepshow." In Screen World 1983. New York: Crown, 1984.

----------. "Cujo." in Screen World 1984. New York: Crown, 1984.

----------. "The Dead Zone." In Screen World 1984. New York: Crown, 1984. Pictorial Review.

Wilson, F. Paul. "TZ Terror." Twilight Zone Magazine (December 1985).

Wilson, William. "Riding the Crest of the Horror Craze." New York Times Magazine 11 May 1980.

Winter, Douglas E. "The Art of Darkness." In Shadowings. Ed. Douglas E. Winter. Mercer Island, WA: Starmont House.

----------. Excerpt from The Faces of Fear. In Castle Rock (May 1985).

----------. "The Funhouse of Fear." Fanatasy Review 95 (October 1986).

----------. "I Want My Cake! Thoughts on Creepshow and E.C. Comics." In Shadowings. Ed. Douglas E. Winter. Mercer Island, WA: Starmont House, 1983.

----------. Review of Pet Sematary. Washington Post Book World 13 November 1983.

----------. "Shadowings: Firestarter by Stephen King." Fantasy Newsletter 30 (November 1980).

----------. "Stephen King, Peter Straub, and the Quest for The Talisman." Twilight Zone Magazine (January/February 1985).

----------. "Stephen King's Christine: ...where innocence peels away like burnt rul. and death rides shotgun." Fanstasy Newsletter 56 (February 1983).

----------. "Stephen King's Cujo: 'Nope, nothing wrong here.'" Fantasy Newsletter 42 (November 1981).

----------. "Thoughts on Creepshow and E.C. Comics." Fantasy Newsletter 56 (February 1983); revised in Shadowings. Ed. Douglas E. Winter. Mercer Island, WA: Starmont House, 1983.

----------. "Winter Reviews Skeleton Crew." Castle Rock (September 1985). Originally appeared in the Philadelphia Inquirer 30 June 1985.

Winters, T. "Brand Name Horror." New York Times Book Review 88 (1983).

Wolf, William. "The Dream Master." New York 9 July 1980.

Wood, Robin. "Cat and Dog: Lewis Teague's Stephen King Novels." Action 2 (Fall 1985).

----------. "King Meets Cronenberg." Canadian Forum (January 1984).

Woods, Larry D. Review of *The Dark Tower: The Gunslinger*. *Science Fiction & Fantasy Book Review* (SFRA) 11 (January-February 1983).

----------. "Stephen King Horrifies Again." *Nashville Tennessean* 25 December 1984.

Wynorski, Jim. "A New Definition for Ultimate Horror: *The Shining*." *Fangoria* (August 1980).

Yardley, Jonathan. "Mean Machine." *Washington Post* 23 March 1983.

INDEX

Before the Play, 54
Bettelheim, Bruno, 4-5
"Birthmark, The," 63-64
black characters, 86-88
Blackwood, Algernon, ii
Blake, William, 67
Body, The, 84-85
Breathing Method, The
97-100, 105
Carrie, 45-47
characterization, 23-24
children, 81-82, 86
Christine, 22-23,
51-52
Cleanup, The, 69
Collector, The, 106,
113-119
Collings, Michael, iv, 87
Collins, Jackie, 81
Cook, Reginald, 60
Cooper, James Fenimore, 87
critics (on King's work), i
Cujo, 96

Danse Macabre, 14-
15, 23, 50-51, 57, 72,
109, 120
Dead Zone, 12-14
Deamer, Robert, 64
Eller, Jackie, 93,
96
Elliott lecture, i
Emerson, Ralph
Waldo, 58
"Ethan Brand," 60-
62
evil, in King's
work, 14, 20, 25-26,
57-67, 79, 119-120
Faulkner, William, 76
Fiedler, Leslie, 8
Firestarter, 30
Frankenstein, 15
free will/deter-
minism, 15-23
Gothicism, 4
government, 29-31

154

Hatlen, Burton, 10, 13, 104
Hawthorne, Nathaniel, 26, 57-67
Heldreth, Leonard, 107
Herron, Donald, 1-2
high schools, 7, 45-47
horror genre, 4-8, 14-15, 50, 68
"Imagery and the Third Eye," 6, 9
Indick, Ben, 7
It, 13, 42, 90, 94-95, 108-112
Jackson, Shirley, ii
Jacob, W.W., ii
Kael, Pauline, 9
Keats, John, 44
King and the Corpse, The, 59
King, Nellie, 91
King, Tabitha, 91-92, 104
Krantz, Judith, 81
Kubrick, Stanley, 108
Le Fanu, Sheridan, ii

Lewis, C.S., 106
Lord of the Flies, 33
machines, 28-37
Maine (setting), 9-14
Martin, Terence, 63
McCammon, Robert, 8
Melville, Herman, 87
Misery, i-ii, 104, 113-119
Mist, The, 28-37, 42
Monteleone, Thomas, 24
morality, 85-89, 106, 112, 119-120
"My Kinsman, Major Molineux," 65
Notkin, Deborah, 1-2
nuclear war, 3-4, 27-28

O'Connor, Flannery, 3
parenthood, 85, 89-92, 98, 103-104
<u>Pet Sematary</u>, 10-11, 58-67
Poe, Edgar Allan, 120
popular fiction, 8-9
prehistoric references, 34, 39-40
Puritans, the, 14, 58-61, 79-80, 108
"Raft, The," iii
"Rappaccini's Daughter," 63
<u>Roadwork</u>, 41
Robinson, E.A., 13
"Roger Malvin's Burial," 59-61
<u>'Salem's Lot</u>, 13, 43, 57, 90, 112-113
<u>Scarlet Letter, The</u> 59-60
sexuality, 42-56, 97-98, 103
Sheldon, Sidney, 81

shine, the, 82-84
<u>Shining, The</u>, 6-7, 15-22, 54-56, 82-84, 90-91, 96, 107-108
<u>Stand, The</u>, 13-14, 35-36, 43, 47-50, 68-78, 94-95, 100-103
Steinbeck, John, 88-89
"Strawberry Spring," 44-45
<u>Talisman, The</u>, 38-41, 85-89
technology, 27-41, 72, 76-77
Thoreau, Henry David, 58
Tolkein, J.R.R., 106
"Trucks, 28-37
Twain, Mark, 87
Underwood, Tim, ii-iv, 6

Walpole, Horace, 4

Wilde, Oscar, ii

wilderness, as symbol, 58-59, 61-67

Winter, Douglas, iv, 27, 81, 91, 112

woman characters, 51, 82, 91, 100-112

"Young Goodman Brown," 57, 61-62

Zimmer, Heinrich, 59

www.ingramcontent.com/pod-product-compliance
Lightning Source LLC
LaVergne TN
LVHW041623070426
835507LV00008B/420